# Supporting Young Transgender Men

*of related interest*

Counseling Transgender and Non-Binary Youth
The Essential Guide
*Irwin Krieger*
ISBN 978 1 78592 743 0
eISBN 978 1 78450 482 3

Counselling Skills for Working with Gender Diversity and Identity
*Michael Beattie and Penny Lenihan with Robin Dundas*
ISBN 978 1 78592 741 6
eISBN 978 1 78450 481 6

Trans Voices
Becoming Who You Are
*Declan Henry*
*Foreword by Professor Stephen Whittle OBE*
*Afterword by Jane Fae*
ISBN 978 1 78592 240 4
eISBN 978 1 78450 520 2

How to Understand Your Gender
A Practical Guide for Exploring Who You Are
*Alex Iantaffi and Meg-John Barker*
*Foreword by S. Bear Bergman*
ISBN 978 1 78592 746 1
eISBN 978 1 78450 517 2

# Supporting Young Transgender Men

## A Guide for Professionals

*Matthew Waites*

Jessica Kingsley *Publishers*
London and Philadelphia

First published in 2018
by Jessica Kingsley Publishers
73 Collier Street
London N1 9BE, UK
and
400 Market Street, Suite 400
Philadelphia, PA 19106, USA

*www.jkp.com*

**Library of Congress Cataloging in Publication Data**
A CIP catalog record for this book is available from the Library of Congress

**British Library Cataloguing in Publication Data**
A CIP catalogue record for this book is available from the British Library

ISBN 978 1 78592 294 7
eISBN 978 1 78450 601 8

Printed and bound in the United States

# Contents

# Preface

Gender dysphoria is defined by the NHS (2017) as the following:

*A condition where a person experiences discomfort or distress because there is a mismatch between their biological sex and gender identity. This is sometimes known as gender identity disorder or gender incongruence.*

Gender dysphoria is complex and still quite new to the scientific world. There is no concrete evidence as to what causes gender dysphoria, only theory; however, it is widely accepted as a medical condition in the UK. There is much controversy around the issue especially when children and young people present with the symptoms of gender dysphoria. There are many debates around ethics as to whether you should treat transgender children and whether they are old enough and have capacity to make their own decisions on their gender identity, especially those that may affect them long term.

For years, gender dysphoria was regarded as a mental health issue; however, research has led to it now being regarded as a medical condition that is usually alleviated by medical intervention and treatment using hormone therapy and surgery.

This book serves as a guide to explore the main issues and challenges that young transgender men face. It is not an explanation of why gender dysphoria occurs, nor is it a discussion of the ethical debates of treating children and young people. The book explains our responsibilities as professionals to young people who identify as transgender and what the law states we have to comply with.

# Terminology

First, it's important to establish that the following definitions are not intended to label people; they are solely for the purpose of putting the following chapters into context and aiding understanding for professionals. Not all trans men will identify with the following definitions and may even have their own definitions for themselves, so when referring to transgender young people it's important that we establish how they like to identify themselves and what they identify with in order to ensure that we promote positive mental health and healthy emotional wellbeing. If we refer to young people in terms that they do not identify with, then this can invalidate their identity and cause emotional harm.

Some of the following definitions are organic in nature; as our society changes so does the language that we use to describe people/items that are associated with developing communities and cultures.

**Binary** – Male or female.

**Binding** – The method that transgender men use in order to flatten their chest. Transgender men can use a variety of binding techniques (some of which will be explored in detail later). There are specific companies that provide compression vests/binders in order to provide transgender people with a more masculine-looking chest in order to 'pass'.

**Cisgender** – Relating to a person whose sense of personal identity and gender corresponds with their assigned sex.

**Gender dysphoria** – The condition of feeling one's emotional and psychological identity as male or female to be the opposite of one's assigned sex.

**Gender fluid** – A term used to describe someone who feels that their gender identity is fluid and can change depending on their feelings.

**Non-binary** – A term used to describe a person who does not identify fully with being male nor with being female (transmasculine and transfeminine are possible terms that a non-binary person identifies with as a result).

**Packing** – The method that transgender men use in order to give the impression that they have a penis. This can be created by a variety of means; however, it is usually achieved by wearing a 'packer', the most common of which is a silicone penis worn in their underwear.

**Passing** – The term used to describe someone's gender expression being accepted by the public; for example, a young person who is a transgender male being referred to as a man in the outside world by people they come across in their day-to-day lives. Being called 'sir' by a member of the public would mean a young person is 'passing' as a male in society.

**Stealth** – Living stealth is a term used to describe a person who is living as a man but whose identity as a transgender man is not known to most people outside of their immediate family/friends.

**Trans man** – A term used to describe a person who was born biologically female and wishes to transition either socially, medically or both to the male gender.

**Transmasculine** – A term used to describe transgender people who were assigned female at birth, but identify with masculinity to a greater extent than with femininity.

**Transgender** – Denoting or relating to a person whose sense of personal identity and gender does not correspond with their assigned sex.

# Chapter 1

# INTRODUCTION

Would you know what to do if a young person you had been working with came to you and told you they thought they might be transgender? Would you know what to do if someone told you they think they should have been a man? Would you know what it meant when that young person tells you that when they look in the mirror, what looks back at them doesn't make sense? Would you know what to do next?

When conversing with other professionals, I've found that their first reactions are a mixed bag of feelings. When asked 'what are the first few things that would go through your mind if a young person told you they were transgender?', some of these professionals shared the following with me:

'You've got a tough road ahead!'

'I'll have to find a service for you as I'm not sure how to help.'

'But you're going to grow up to become a beautiful woman, why wouldn't you want that?'

It's common for professionals to go through a rollercoaster of emotions when put on the spot by a young person. We've all been there and that's OK! But we need to remember that we are there to serve that young person throughout their journey and ensure that we as workers protect them, make sure they gain all the support and treatment they need and are entitled to and create an environment where they feel safe to be themselves. It's quite a responsibility to have, but it's important to remember that regardless of your opinion on the matter, you still need to ensure that you set in motion a person-centred strategy to obtain the best possible outcome for that young person.

Lack of knowledge makes people feel uncomfortable and it's that uncomfortable feeling that shapes people's practices. In some cases these practices are outdated, unprofessional and damaging to young people's mental health and emotional wellbeing; that's why we'll be addressing these issues in the following chapters.

It's OK to be unsure about how to support a transgender young person and it's also OK to be honest about that uncertainty. However, it is not OK to use language, facial expressions and derogatory tones towards or about trans young people even if the subject matter does make you uncomfortable. This is unsafe practice, and if transgender young people cannot gain support from a professional who has a legal obligation to support them, then who do they turn to?

In a survey I conducted using SurveyMonkey of 18 professionals working in a variety of frontline sectors from social services and probation services to homeless services for young people and generic youth and community services, I found the following:

- Sixty-seven per cent of participants felt somewhat confident in supporting transgender young men, while 22 per cent felt very confident and 11 per cent felt not at all confident in supporting transgender men through their journeys.

- Thirty-three per cent of respondents felt that they had enough knowledge to be able to support transgender young men and advise them on issues relating to transition, while 50 per cent said they didn't. Seventeen per cent stated that with training and education they would feel they had the right knowledge and expertise to support transgender young men.

Respondents identified the following as the biggest issues hindering frontline professionals in supporting transgender men through transition:

- lack of training

- lack of knowledge, insight and experience

- lack of education, resources and support

- lack of mental health services for under-25s

- society and awareness.

Of the 18 professionals asked, one participant stated that they had been on specific training addressing the needs of transgender men and the barriers they face. The remaining participants had received no training.

Forty-four per cent of professionals felt that they would know how to access advice and guidance for young people they were supporting, with 56 per cent stating they would not know who to turn to.

Half of the identified professionals group felt that they were confident in using specific terminology when addressing issues relating to transition, and half felt not at all confident. One participant stated:

'I feel like I would be "walking on eggshells" trying not to say the wrong thing.' Anonymous

Twenty-seven per cent of professionals asked said they felt confident in their understanding of the NHS treatment systems and how to obtain medical support for young people, with 73 per cent stating that they did not have up-to-date and relevant knowledge on how young people started their physical transition and what path they needed to take in order to receive treatment. Only two members of the group felt that they had a good understanding of the differences between NHS treatment options and private treatment options.

This guide will aim to address the needs of professionals by providing up-to-date knowledge on the subject to ensure that all frontline professionals working with young people in any sector know how to support transgender young people on their path to personal discovery and their journey through transition. The book will focus on mental health, the impact that being transgender can have on young people's mental health and what we as professionals, regardless of sector, can do to support and serve the transgender community.

# Chapter 2

# GENDER DEVELOPMENT IN CHILDREN

It is important to note that transgender identities don't just come out of thin air once a young person hits a certain age; S. Brill and R. Pepper's research suggests that young people can identify as gender non-conforming from as young as two or three years. The researchers explain in their book *The Transgender Child* (2008) that children have a sense of gender from the ages of between two and three years and by the age of three they start to order their life and they can understand differences between men and women based on stereotypical appearances, for example hair length and voice pitch. Children understand the difference between gendered toys and will align themselves with peers and toys that reflect their gender identity. The same is said of transgender children; they too will align themselves with peers and toys that they find reflect their gender identity, and this is when parents and other adults in the child's life may start to realise that their child is gender non-conforming and starting to identify as the opposite gender to their assigned sex. It is important to emphasise that it is society that places gender roles on toys. Trans boys may wish to play with toys that society recognises as 'girls" toys and that's OK too. The less restrictive professionals and parents are with exploring play, the more likely the child's emotional wellbeing will be protected, leading to healthy growth and development.

With this in mind, it's important to be supportive of children at such a young age. Allowing them to play with toys that are typically associated with the opposite gender is absolutely fine; nothing bad will result from this. Take each day as it comes and, in responding to the child, take your cues from them. If they want to play with the boys, don't discourage it; if they want to play with 'boys" toys, again don't discourage it, because doing so can cause emotional harm.

By expressing your concerns about children playing with toys that aren't stereotypically associated with their assigned sex, you will send the message that playing with those toys/playing with children of a certain gender is not OK and you will start to create an environment where self-exploration is not acceptable and not understood. Children will begin to learn that being different is not OK and playing with toys that 'aren't for them' may invoke feelings of shame, which is damaging to a child's self-esteem and development. Professionals have a key role in providing a safe space for all children and young people, and discouraging certain behaviours based on social stereotypes is emotionally damaging for a child. The impact may not be seen until the teenage years or adulthood; however, the more you insist a child conforms to behaviours associated with their assigned sex, the greater the damage that will be done further down the line. The child will start to feel ashamed of and embarrassed by their behaviour, and this is a message that will stick with them and that usually contributes to the fear that young transgender men face when they start to decide whether or not to come out (see Chapter 3). The consequences of fear can be detrimental, so it's important to provide a safe and encouraging space for children to be free to explore their identities.

Supporting social transition in primary school years is a topic of discussion that is controversial and debatable.

Should we let children be who they say they are? Do they really know who they are at such a young age?

At the age of three to four years gender in children starts to become more refined; children develop a deeper understanding of what male and female means and can develop stereotypes for the two binary groups. The child's knowledge and understanding of gender identity becomes more refined up until the age of 12, by when they have a deeper understanding of gender and what it means to be a man or a woman. Complexities occur when children at this age understand that they are biologically male or female but identify more with the opposite gender, and that's where professionals will start to see the symptoms of gender dysphoria. For some children this experience is more intense than it is for others, and adults' reactions to children when they start to show signs of gender non-conformity will shape a child's feelings on gender identity and what it means to be transgender once they have the knowledge and language to describe how they feel. Non-acceptance of gender non-conformity will induce feelings of shame, fear and rejection, whereas accepting gender non-conformity will build self-esteem, confidence and a strong sense of self-worth for the child, including a strong association with their preferred gender and therefore feelings of being more comfortable in their own body.

Parents may be afraid that by 'encouraging' gender non-conforming behaviour they will make their child transgender: the standard nature vs nurture debate. Emphasise nurturing the child in your life. If they are visibly distressed by your actions, correct your behaviour and encourage children to wear and do what makes them happy.

A child with gender dysphoria will have it whether or not a parent accepts it. Studies suggesting parental influence on gender dysphoria have been widely disputed. What parents can influence is how a young person develops from that point, shaping their mental health and emotional wellbeing for the future.

Take your cues from the child; if they want to be called a different name or be called he, then what's the worst that will happen if you allow that? What's the worst that will happen if you let them wear clothes associated with the opposite gender to that they were born? No medical professional in the United Kingdom is going to assess a child as transgender, pump them full of hormones and then put them on an operating table for gender reassignment surgery. There are strict criteria for receipt of hormone therapy and surgical procedures as per current NHS Interim Gender Dysphoria Protocol and Service Guidelines (Department of Health 2013/14), and these are discussed in later chapters.

Other children may bully trans children, but the issue then is that some children are bullying other children and that's an issue that is dealt with through the school's bullying policy and dealt with as any other bullying incident would be.

Speak to the non-conforming child's parents: what do they want to happen? Have they done some research? Point them in the direction of relevant and up-to-date information so that they can make an informed decision and make a commitment to supporting their child in the best way possible.

Remember, we are there as professionals to serve our communities; it is our job to make sure that children and young people are safe and free from harm. If a child is clearly upset because they are not able to be themselves, ask yourself what happens when you let them dress in the clothes they want to dress in or you allow them to go by a different name. Do they present as happier? If so, then that's what you work towards. A happier child.

If you're concerned that parents feel they are acting in the best interest of the child by not letting them dress or act the way they want to, then refer them to groups specifically for parents of transgender children so that they can learn more and make up their minds from there. Parents may feel frightened for their child and automatically want to protect them, causing them to force the child into a gender role that they don't want to be in, causing more harm than good.

This is the child's journey and you're along to help navigate in the direction that they want to go in. It is their life and they have to live in their bodies day in, day out. As a professional, it is your job to ensure that they are safe and protected from harm; it is clear that when a young person is free to be themselves they thrive, and that is evident in our everyday practice. When they're afraid to be who they really are, those thoughts take precedence in their minds, preventing them from engaging fully in education or other aspects of their life.

# Chapter 3

# SOCIAL TRANSITION

## COMING OUT

When a young person decides that they will come out, they've usually been thinking of how they will do it, who they will tell first and what's going to happen once those significant people have been told. They will have been thinking about this moment for months or even years, and the fear that they've been experiencing will come to a head. Trans young men might present to workers with a range of emotions from anger, fear and tearfulness to liberation and relief. It's an emotional process for the young person to go through, but almost a rite of passage, following in the footsteps of those that have gone before them, putting their lives on the line and, in some cases, revealing that one big secret that people knew was there…but just didn't know what it was. We all have parts of our lives that we don't share with our colleagues and parts of our lives that we don't share with our friends and families, and usually for good reason. For a transgender young person though, coming out is something that everyone in their lives needs to know, so they cannot pick and choose who to tell if they decide they want to live full time as their desired gender. For a trans young person who considers their transition to be their secret, it is likely they will experience high levels of anxiety before coming out, and this can present itself in some of the following ways:

- avoiding situations where they may have to be split by gender, for example sports groups

- becoming distant from friends, family or those that they consider to be close to them

- anger

- depression

- social isolation.

It's important to note that not all trans men will feel that they have a secret to keep, and in some cases it was the path to discovery that was proving to be the most difficult task together with trying to find the words to explain how they identified in order to present to the outside world. The young person may therefore present as very confident in coming out and ready to take on the world, but it's important that they understand that unfortunately their world may not be ready to hear what they have to say.

For most trans men, prior to coming out their mental health is suffering. They're living with something that nobody knows about and they cannot identify a safe person to disclose to, therefore there is no one supporting them specifically with being transgender.

When we're upset, we turn to people to share our problems with, to discuss what we can do about them and find a solution that works for us. We're social beings, and as a consequence we surround ourselves with people who understand us and can support us in our time of need. Trans men, prior to coming out, don't have this support network (unless they're accessing trans-specific support groups), and so mental health can deteriorate quite rapidly and leave people feeling socially isolated, depressed, anxious and suicidal. For some people, that's the reality of being transgender. From my own personal experience of being transgender and consulting with other transgender men, I can tell you that before making the decision to come out, trans men have considered the following (in no particular order):

- What will school/college/work say?

- Am I likely to lose my family?

- Which toilets will I use when I'm at school/college/work?

- Is it worth it?

- Maybe I can keep this under wraps and just live as a woman. Everyone will be happier, and it won't cause destruction. Even though I'll be unhappy, the sacrifice might be worth it, in order to keep the things that I value secure.

- What if I lose my place at school/work/college?

- Will I be made homeless?

- Will I ever find a partner? Being transgender will compromise my chances of doing so.

- Am I doing this so that I can get ahead in the career market?

- There's nothing wrong with identifying as a woman, so why do I feel it isn't for me?

Trans men will consider these questions with a heavy heart, and these are the things that they will be facing every day of their life prior to coming out. Gender stereotypes are everywhere within society, so there is a constant reminder of the subject, which takes its toll on mental health and emotional wellbeing.

Ultimately it is the young person's choice as to whether or not they come out and/or transition. Every transgender person has a choice about how they go about transition. They can either transition socially or physically or not at all, and each of these decisions is acceptable. It is important to consider the impact on mental health that being transgender and not transitioning can have on a young person and ensure that we follow safeguarding best practice in order to protect young people from harm, regardless of which option they take.

Deciding to transition is a life-changing decision to make and the considerations above will not be taken lightly. In most cases, trans men get to a point in their lives when they are ready to make a big sacrifice if necessary in order to become who they truly are. Ultimately they are emotionally and psychologically ready for the losses they may face because they value transition more highly than having a job or even a family in some cases. This is because of the prolonged psychological torture the person has been through in keeping this a secret for so long. The decision to come out is a significant step on their journey to discovering themselves, but there comes a point where transgender men have to make a decision about how to move forward and embrace the future, no matter what is thrown at them.

> 'I feared being seen as disgusting, I feared not being accepted; although my parents are very supportive and non-judgemental, it was a bigger step coming out as transgender compared to when I initially came out as a lesbian.' Anonymous, 18 years old

Often young people will come to a crossroads, at which point they feel that they only have two choices left:

1. come out – embrace being transgender (with or without medical intervention) and live as who I truly am

2. suicide.

In a study conducted by the charity PACE and reported by *The Guardian* (Strudwick 2014) 48 per cent of transgender young people under the age of 26 had attempted suicide. Fifty-nine per cent of transgender youth stated they had at least considered suicide in comparison to 6 per cent of all 16–24-year-olds who had attempted suicide.

'I felt suicidal as a direct response to being transgender, I struggled with being unhappy in my body and I knew it would take a long time to get where I wanted to be.' Trans man, 18 years old

The statistics are shocking, and that's why, when a transgender young person comes out to you, it's likely they have made the decision to live. The professional has a responsibility at this point to be sensitive and accepting towards the young person. If you're the first person they've come out to, they're looking for support and they need an ally. If young people fall at the first hurdle because the professional that they have disclosed to has reacted in an unprofessional manner, then there is an increased risk of suicide. Imagine telling someone your secret and being rejected by them. How would you feel?

Empathy is an important part of supporting a young person through transition. Being open minded to learning about transition and being willing to support a young person through transition is enough to save a life. We don't have to have all the answers, and it's OK to ask questions that are sensitive around the topic area in order to learn and further support the young person you're working with. Most young people will accept that it is not a topic that is widely discussed in day-to-day working life, nor is it something that we come across daily unless working directly with transgender young people as a targeted group. It's OK to tell a young person that you will need to do some research in order to try and support them further, and nine times out of ten you'll have a positive response because you've demonstrated your ability to be flexible to their needs and your willingness to support them through a significant phase of their life.

Some young people may have people in their lives already that they know would be supportive towards them and accepting of who they are when they have come out to them. It is likely to be a very positive and liberating experience for a young person to come out to someone who is fully accepting of their trans status and makes a commitment to support them. So, if a young person has these people in their lives already, why not consider telling them first? It's not always appropriate to tell parents/carers first. Building up a supportive network is essential to preserving life, and so supporting a young person to identify safe people to tell first will ensure that the young person starts to build a support network which is essential for maintaining positive mental health and emotional wellbeing. If a young person can identify these key people, it is likely that they will be able to turn to them in times of crisis and know that they will get the right support, especially when professionals aren't around to be the protective factor.

Mental health is affected significantly prior to young people coming out as transgender. The suicide rates are higher as transgender men feel desperate and unsure about how they will continue their lives ahead. Depression and anxiety are sometimes diagnosed prior to coming out, and young people are more likely to obtain mental health support through their GP before coming out in order to help them reach an emotional state for dealing with day-to-day life.

'My mental health prior to coming out was poor. I was diagnosed with depression and anxiety and, after speaking with a psychiatrist, managed to shed light on how much my gender identity impacted my mental health. It affected my relationships with people because I feared rejection and I often wished to hang around with the lads, but I always knew I was different and so

did others; which led to being bullied mostly throughout my school life, which really affected my mental health.'
Anonymous

Transgender men described a variety of responses from people around them when they came out, from rejection and isolation from family and friends to being fully accepted as who they are. Some transgender men explained that their parents felt that they had died and they therefore mourned the loss of someone who was still alive; they went through a grieving process before accepting who their child was and supporting them.

The first conversation that a young person has about their gender identity will be key to whether or not they have decided to trust you to support them. It is likely that young people may 'dip their toe in the water' to find out what your opinions are on transgender people. They may start a conversation by referring to something they have watched or may even make up scenarios about something that they witnessed to test your response and establish whether or not you are a 'safe' person to tell.

It is crucial at this point that you build the foundations required in order for a young person to feel safe in confiding in you and also to ensure that they fully understand that you will be there to support them, without pushing them to come out to you. It's quite a balance to strike. Use appropriate and positive language, and use real life examples, perhaps referring to celebrities and their experiences in order to help build rapport. Inform young people that you understand transgender issues, and use examples to back up that knowledge.

In order to ensure that young people feel safe at your service, you may want to consider using posters/leaflets or even young person-friendly policies that directly address transgender young people to inform them that they are in a safe space. Can you build up a network of colleagues who wear pin badges or lanyards that clearly identify them as professionals who are understanding of transgender people's needs?

Do you have a toilet that is gender neutral? Put a poster on the toilet door that refers to that particular bathroom being gender neutral. Although it won't specifically shout out 'we're not transphobic', it shows that you are educated professionals who understand the needs of transgender young people. There are lots of resources that you can use from organisations such as Stonewall; for example, you can buy posters to display to evidence that your services are trans friendly, and if all else fails, you can always make your own poster!

These strategies are quite subtle but they will send the message that should be conveyed by every project providing services to young people. The message is one of education, compassion, safety and knowledge, and that is a powerful message to send. When young people feel that the time is right, you will be the person they are confiding in, which is quite a privilege to have.

## THE GRIEVING PROCESS AND THE IMPACT OF PARENTAL RESPONSE

Parents can find themselves in a difficult situation when their child first tells them that they want to transition. They often explain that they saw it coming but didn't want to accept it until they no longer had a choice. In an interview with one parent, who requests to remain anonymous, they described a feeling of grieving for their lost child:

'I still grieve the loss of my daughter. I'm sad for the things that will never be: prom dresses, wedding, children. My daughter was exceptionally pretty and I am secretly thrilled when I see glimpses of her female self. I feel like she's an unexceptional man.' Parent of a 16-year-old trans man

Grief is a complex process and it's important to recognise that it is different for everyone. The five stages of grief is a model that is tried and tested and that a lot of people can recognise; however, we need to remember that grief is individual and parents will experience a wide range of emotions when they are grieving the loss of a child that hasn't died.

Some parents report that they felt that their child had died. If we consider the traumatic experience of what would happen to a parent if their child had in fact died, then we can empathise with the trauma they may be going through. This will manifest itself in a variety of ways, and the range of emotions experienced can impact on mental health, which in turn can impact on a child's development, self-esteem and confidence. Equally, parents may abandon their children, turning them over to the state for care, which in itself has its own consequences for all involved.

In working with a parent/family that is going through this process with their child, it is essential that we encourage self-reflection and a healthy grieving process. We cannot take away the pain that a parent may be feeling; we can however ensure a better outcome for our service users.

Encourage the parent to talk about their feelings with someone who can look at the situation objectively. For example, this person may be able to convey that it wouldn't be advisable for the parent to tell a child that they felt they had died, because this would contribute to feelings of isolation and non-existence within the family, thereby impacting on self-esteem. It may be worth suggesting talking to a counsellor, or is there a local parents of transgender children group that could provide support?

Suggest to the parent that they do some research. There is plenty of information on the internet and this is the place that most people start when they are trying to gain further understanding and knowledge but don't yet have the confidence to approach a professional. It's important to stress that information should come from credible sources; there are charities that can support parents of transgender children (see Resources), but some are better than others and some are dangerous.

At this point, I would like to touch upon the impact of conversion therapy (reparation therapy) on gender non-conforming children and how this affects their psychological and emotional development.

The UK Council for Psychotherapy (2014) defines conversion therapy as 'a type of talking therapy or activity that is aimed at changing/repairing gender dysphoria'. The Council also explains that there is no credible evidence to show that this type of therapy works but it can cause significant harm.

The National Centre for Lesbian Rights explains the findings from its #BornPerfect campaign (2017). It found that the risk of practising conversion therapy can lead to depression, guilt, helplessness, hopelessness, shame, social withdrawal, suicidal ideation, substance abuse, stress, disappointment, self-blame and decreased self-esteem and authenticity to others. It reports that conversion therapy can increase self-hatred, blame and hostility towards parents and feelings of anger and betrayal. The evidence speaks for itself.

You may think that conversion therapy is an outdated practice that doesn't really happen any more; however, there is currently no law in the UK that bans conversion therapy. It is still legal for professionals to practise this. Stonewall explains in its *Unhealthy Attitudes* report (Summerville 2015) that in order for conversion therapy to take place within the NHS or other public professional providers of psychotherapy, this treatment has to be evidence based. It is condemned by major professional bodies, from the Royal College of Psychiatry to the British Psychological Society. This doesn't stop some people from offering this type of therapy because, as discussed, it is not illegal.

If you're concerned about a family that are considering conversion therapy, explain to them the impact and dangers of doing so. It is advisable that you consult your local safeguarding board, because as the evidence above suggests, it can cause significant harm to mental health, emotional wellbeing and the development of a child.

As professionals, most of us will have had our run-ins with social services, and have found it difficult to engage social services when we believe the stakes to be high. However, it is important you remain consistent, outline your concerns, back them up with evidence from the numerous studies that have been done, include that major professional bodies have condemned the practice and state your case. It will be difficult for social services to say no to you if you have made a watertight case for them to consider. Ultimately, a child is at significant risk of harm regardless of our personal opinions and whether or not conversion therapy is legal, and that should be at the very core of their investigation and our concerns.

## OVERCOMING FEAR AND EMPOWERING YOUNG PEOPLE

Many young people will be suffering with some level of fear and anxiety with regards to coming out. Fear is an overwhelming emotion that can cripple and debilitate anyone who feels it. It acts as a barrier to obtaining what we truly want and is so powerful that it can stop us from achieving our goals. With the barrier of fear hindering our progression, mental health can deteriorate because we get stuck in the 'vicious circle'. The vicious circle is defined by the Cambridge English Dictionary as being 'a continuing and unpleasant situation, created when one problem causes another problem, that then makes the first problem worse'. So, in this context, let's consider a young person who is starting to think about coming out to their parents and what that experience may look like for them.

They will first start to consider the physical and emotional impacts of coming out. The young person will consider whether their parents/caregivers may be angry, upset or annoyed; coming out may result in abuse. Young people may imagine losing their home and their family, who they rely on to meet their emotional and physical needs. They may then consider the positive emotions of the possibility of feeling liberated, being supported by their loved ones and living as their true selves.

What follows then is a balancing act of attempting to determine which situation would hold the better outcome. Now, at this point you may be thinking it's quite straightforward: 'Of course the better outcome is to live as your true self and be supported in doing so.' However, for a young person experiencing the vicious circle, the better outcome has to be the one that is the least damaging for *all* the people involved in their life, which may or may not include the impact on themselves. The outcome can be determined by many factors such as the personalities, and the political affiliations, religion, morals, ethics and values, of the people in their life.

So, if a young person feels that they may be a victim of abuse because they identify as trans and they decide that having to endure the pain of abuse would be less favourable than coming out, then their decision will be not to come out. They may be wondering if their parents will be disappointed in them, and they have to consider whether or not they can deal with the pain disappointment may bring, all while trying to grapple with the intense fear of the unknown. This results in the young person becoming stuck in the vicious circle. Therefore, the continuing unpleasant situation results from the pain and trauma suffered when the young person realises that they are trans but feels that they cannot come out because coming out may then create another problem. The impact of fearing what may happen to them after coming out results in making the initial problem worse than it already was. This can have significant impact on the young person's mental health and emotional wellbeing.

It is a traumatising thought process for a young person to go through and results in them being fearful of what might happen. In some cases, it is at this point in their lives that they may start to consider suicide. Being transgender can be seen as a problem in a young person's mind, and if a young person considers that coming out will make it worse, then the alternative for them may be to consider suicide as a way out. The young person may feel that the pain of keeping it a secret is already becoming unbearable, and fear that it will only get worse exacerbates this pain. Fear fuels the fire and then determines what action a young person may take.

If the young person feels they cannot overcome the fear they are feeling and they then decide to continue to keep their gender dysphoria a secret, harbouring that secret comes with its own price, and that is when a young person's mental health and emotional wellbeing will start to suffer and you may see the visual symptoms of deteriorating mental health, or may even be dealing with a suicidal young person.

So, what's next? How do we as practitioners preserve life when this situation happens? We may have seen subtle hints that the young person has thrown at us; they may have tested the water with us and talked about transgender friends, for example. If we're noticing signs and symptoms of deteriorating mental health and emotional wellbeing, then maybe it's time to consider being brave and putting our hypothesis on their gender identity to the test.

I'm not talking about going to see a young person all guns blazing and just throwing it out there and asking if they're transgender; you'll need to use your professional judgement and treat the situation with delicacy and sensitivity. Not all young men who are struggling with their mental health will be considering their gender identity. However, if you're seeing the signs that a young person is suffering and you're confident that they may be dealing with gender identity issues, you may find yourself in a situation where you feel they could be close to disclosing what the issues are. It may be that they cannot find the words to tell you or that they aren't brave enough because they're very afraid to say what's really going on. Once people have figured out what's happening and it's out in the big wide world that they are gender dysphoric, it becomes very real, and that is a daunting prospect. Sensitivity and empathy are vital.

One of two things will happen if you ask a young person if they are struggling with their gender identity:

1.  They will deny it.

2.  They will confirm it.

Whatever their response, by asking the question you're providing the young person with a safe space to come out. Reassure them that sharing information with regards to gender identity is confidential and explain that you'll only disclose that information if they are at risk of harm.

Talk about the topic of gender diversity openly and in a generic way. Make sure that you are clear that it is OK to talk about it, that the world hasn't ended (using words appropriate to the situation) and that you'll be there for them when they're ready to talk. Always have an open door policy and advise your colleagues of your concerns. If your colleagues require further knowledge on the subject, then point them in the right direction (see Resources). Be prepared; if you're the one a young person comes out to, you never know – you may have saved a life.

It may be considered quite drastic action to openly ask a young person about their gender identity, but before doing so, consider what could happen if they cannot find a safe person to tell. What's the worst that will happen if you ask them and what's the worst that can happen if you don't?

Already we can understand that there is a lot for a young transgender person to process and deal with, especially when they start to consider the big picture – that's when things will become overwhelming and people will find it difficult to cope with.

Consider completing a session with a young person based on timelines. Identify the key steps that they want to take and work backwards in order to break each one down into manageable goals. This will make information and actions easier to process. Ensure you utilise the SMART way of thinking (Specific, Measurable, Attainable, Realistic and Timebound), which will ensure that the goals set are appropriate, manageable and achievable. Achievement of the 'smaller' goals will empower a young person to continue on their journey towards their own sense of identity. Not every young person will want to transition, so ensure that the timeline is tailored to the service user. It won't be appropriate to follow all the steps from this book if a young person has no interest in physical transition, for example.

## SAFETY PLANNING

Most professionals have had to conduct safety plans for a variety of issues, be it due to a young person being vulnerable to domestic violence, or from other young people, for example, and leading one for a young transgender man will be no different.

It is important to consider a safety plan especially if the young person is fearful that they may be physically/emotionally abused because of their trans status or if they are worried about becoming homeless after telling their parents/carers/relatives. It is important that the professional takes the lead from the young person. If they are genuinely fearful of what may happen next, then a safety plan is a good place to start. As professionals, we're only around for limited times during the week; we can't always be there, for instance, when a young person decides to tell their parents at 9pm on a Friday night, so a safety plan is an essential strategy that will enable them to take control if they find themselves in a vulnerable situation.

There are several things you need to consider when writing a safety plan:

- If a young person becomes homeless during office hours, what can they do?

- If a young person becomes homeless outside of office hours, where can they turn to for support? Who should they contact? Have they got the means to be able to phone someone for support? Give details of emergency accommodation providers, social services duty teams, local provision/night shelters (dependent on the age of the young person you're working with) and so on.

- Are there any friends that the young person can stay with for a short time if they are asked to leave the family home? Can they call those people to prepare them in case they do need somewhere safe to stay?

- Consider how the young person is likely to feel if they are rejected by the people they've come out to. If it is their parents, ask them to imagine what they are likely to experience. Their mental health is likely to be compromised if they are rejected by the very people that brought them into the world, so who can they turn to? Phone numbers for access and crisis teams locally are essential information. Contact details for Samaritans would be a good place to start as they can provide support 24/7. If there are any local mental health providers in your area that offer a 24/7 service, then make sure the young person is given this information too. Also consider giving young people the phone number for the local Children's Services duty team. If they are under 18 then they are likely to require Children's Services intervention if made homeless.

- Is there a safe word that both parties can come up with so that if the young person is feeling suicidal, for example, but doesn't know how to tell you, they can use this word and the professional can start the conversation from there?

- Is self-harm a risk factor? If so, what strategies does the young person have that they use if they are trying to protect themselves from self-harm? Do they know basic first aid in terms of caring for wounds and how to identify when they may need further medical assistance?

- If a young person wants to tell their parents but needs additional support, do you have the space to bring parents into your office and support the young person through that process? Be sure to check your services policies on offering support of this nature. Some services may not feel this is appropriate.

These are some very basic strategies for safety planning, and they are probably similar to other safety plans in other situations. Setting up the safety plan involves a risk assessment: What are the likely risks? What are young people going to face? What can they do when you're not around? Who can they turn to for support? As professionals we have to ensure that we cover every possible scenario in order to preserve life. Give the young person a copy of their safety plan. There's likely to be a lot of information for the young person to remember. Is there a trusted friend/family member the young person can also give a copy of the safety plan to just in case they lose their copy?

Not all young people will want to come out to everyone and may wish to live stealth. When comparing coming out as a transgender man to coming out as a gay person, the latter have the option to either come out or not: not coming out can be a realistic option for them. However, for a transgender man, while living stealth can be a feasible option for some, key people will need to know that he is transitioning; therefore no one can ever truly live a stealth life.

If a young person doesn't wish to come out and live as a transgender man but instead be seen as a man within society, then there may be an option to start a new school/college with their new name and live stealth. It's important to consider all of these options because what's right for one young trans man may not be right for the other. Young people are the experts in their own lives, so it's important that we listen to them and support them with the decisions they make in order to contribute to positive emotional wellbeing and mental health.

Not everyone has to be out, loud and proud or march down the streets holding trans flags campaigning for transgender rights, or give speeches because they are trans. There is a pressure within the community to conform to such behaviour when young people do come out and it's important that we encourage the young person to do what they are comfortable with.

It is important to remember that, by law, transgender people have the right not to be 'outed' by others, and those who do out people can be taken to court under the Equality Act, especially if being outed has directly resulted in a hate crime being committed.

Make sure that you are clear with young people about what they want from you. If they want you to tell people, write down an agreement between yourselves so that all parties are clear on their role and what is expected of the professional. This will create clarity of purpose and ensure that accidents don't happen!

It may also be useful for a young person to consider that if they do choose to be stealth, when they connect with other people and share experiences from their past, they may have to censor some of their experiences in order to not out themselves. For example, if a young person had decided to live stealth and was sharing a story or a part of their life that happened when they lived as female with someone that is not aware of their trans status, they will need to remember to change pronouns for themselves and other details in order to continue living as stealth. For instance, if someone went to an all-girls school and is reliving an experience to someone and refers to the school directly, questions may follow. The young person is then put in a vulnerable position as they either have to answer the questions or cover it up, resulting in discomfort around the topic. It's important to remind young people that living stealth is not about lying to people; it's about making the choices that are right for them. No one likes to 'lie' to their friends/colleagues and everyone wants to live as their authentic selves, and if living stealth means that people can live authentically then that's OK. Censoring our lives and experiences is not particularly pleasant and takes some work, but it's important that we recognise this as an element of living stealth that needs to be considered. We all have different aspects of our personalities that we reveal to different people in different circumstances. Our colleagues may not see our whole personalities because we remain professional and we're there to do a job. Our families will see a different side to us. Living as a stealth trans man comes under similar principles; it's not about lying, it's about living the best version of ourselves that we can be and that we are comfortable with.

It will take time for professionals to adjust to a new name and pronouns for a person, so ensure that you and your team are trying your best to do this. Remind the young person that you are trying your best if you do misgender them and call each other out when people get it wrong so that they are aware of what they're doing and can adjust their behaviour. If we don't know we're doing something that upsets others, then how can we be expected to change our behaviour?

## SOCIAL AFFIRMATION

Social affirmation is the process a young man would go through in order to align his life socially with the gender role he intends to live as. This includes changing his name by deed poll and consequently changing it at places such as the GP, the bank, Passport Office, DVLA and so on. Social affirmation can mean different things to different people. It could be that they change their entire wardrobe, or it could be a name change and coming out. Each individual is different, and therefore social transition is different for everyone. It's important to remember that, and the following chapters encompass many different routes of social affirmation.

Social affirmation starts with passing. Passing is the concept whereby a young person presents themselves as male to the world and the world accepts them as male. The concept is one that can be argued as oppressive in nature due to the fact that passing is generally based on male stereotypes. For some trans men fitting into these stereotypes is very important; for others it can oppress their true nature by not allowing for flexibility in what they wear or their behaviour in social situations. It is important for binary transgender men to be read as male by others that they are likely to encounter in social situations.

For a trans man who is pre hormone therapy, it can be difficult to be read as male by others due to potentially more feminine features. Height can be an issue, and smaller hands, higher voice and an undefined jaw are all things that the people we encounter within the communities we live and work in will use subconsciously to determine someone's gender. They will then adapt their behaviour or language in addressing someone of that gender.

Again, everyone is different: their bodies, behaviour, language and voice pitch. If young people are not being read as their chosen gender, this can have an impact on their mental health and can escalate dysphoria; it can lead to social isolation and anxiety around encountering social situations.

In order to be read as male transgender, young men will tend to hyper masculinise in order to compensate for the features that they don't have that usually tell others what their gender is. They'll cut their hair very short and opt for a very masculine cut, for example. They'll wear what other men their age are wearing and they'll behave in similar ways in order to pass. It is important as practitioners that we encourage young people to genuinely be themselves. We need to remind them that although it can be frustrating that they might not pass all the time in social situations, it's more important that they are comfortable in themselves on a day-to-day basis and with what they are wearing and how they choose to present themselves to the world. However, hyper masculinisation can also be a very liberating thing for a young trans man. To go out into the community with his friends in his new clothes and with his new hair style and be read as male can have a very positive impact on mental health and overall wellbeing.

Individuality is important, and it's vital that we encourage it regardless of the presentation of a young person, be it more androgynous, feminine or masculine. We must still work hard to ensure that we are using the right names and pronouns for the young people that we support. This will have a positive impact on mental health and will subtly remind them that no matter how they present to the world, they are still male; you see that as their support worker and they will see it in themselves over time.

## SOCIAL BEHAVIOUR AND CULTURE
Stereotypically, men and women experience very different social cues and behaviours in different situations. A young trans

man is likely to be trying to understand these in order to feel more masculine and to reinforce his sense of identity.

Generally speaking, most cisgender young men have a few things on their minds when they're growing up. These are usually centred around fitting into social situations, having a group of friends that they belong to, exploring and understanding their bodies through puberty and defying social norms (based on adult perceptions of social norms). We all know that teenagers like to push the boundaries and discover what's acceptable and what's not in difficult social situations. Young transgender men are no different, and they are likely to want to be a part of the social culture that they identify with and experience the same culture that cisgender young men experience. This can be liberating and exciting for a transgender young man; it can also escalate deviant and risk-taking behaviours.

We all feel a need to belong to something or a group of people that we can connect with, and for transgender young men, that's no different. Amongst teenagers, there is generally more risk-taking behaviour as they learn about themselves and find their own paths in life. The risk-taking behaviour that we generally associate with young men includes increased consumption of drugs and alcohol and an increase in social deviancy, including anti-social behaviour and peer pressure. A transgender man who is trying to fit into a community that he feels he belongs to may want to 'prove himself' in order to become a part of the group, and this is the reason why risk-taking behaviour can increase. The need to become 'one of the lads' is greater than the fear of the damaging situations he may find himself in. Symptoms of increased risk-taking behaviour amongst the young trans male community can include, but are not limited to, the following:

- increased alcohol consumption

- increased consumption/experimentation with drugs

- visible bruising/cuts from being involved in fights

- breaking the rules that they are usually not known to break, such as curfew

- being secretive about where they are going and who they are going with

- socialising with older males who they may find more accepting of their gender status.

It is important to note that these risk-taking behaviours are common amongst cisgender young men also and, because of that, transgender young men are more likely to push the boundaries further than that of their cisgender friends. For example, drug consumption amongst cisgender males tends to be centred around trying cannabis. Transgender young men can find themselves trying cannabis and then moving to harder drugs in order to fit in with their group of friends and prove that they belong within that community. Not all transgender men will experience an increase in risk-taking behaviours, but it is important to be aware of the risk factors in order to try to minimise harm and risk to the young people that we support. Referrals to specific drug and alcohol services may help to reduce harm caused in situations like this, as will a referral to an anti-social behaviour programme if your local area provides this.

If the young transgender man finds himself on the wrong side of the law, this can be a very eye-opening experience for him, especially if he has socially transitioned and is living as male. He will be searched by female officers if he is taken into custody, and because the justice system has gender-specific juvenile detention centres, it may be that a young transgender man finds himself in a female prison if his anti-social behaviour has increased to the point where he has been convicted of offences. This will be a traumatising experience for a young transgender man, and has the possibility of severely impacting on mental health. He will have to live with other females in a female juvenile centre; he may be bullied or criticised for his presentation. Unfortunately, there are limited detention centres that are of mixed gender. It is advisable that if you feel this young transgender man is heading towards being incarcerated he is made aware of this information. He needs to be aware of how his behaviour impacts and has consequences in society and even more so for him as a transgender man. He must understand that his behaviour will have a significant impact on his life, as it would with any other young person who is incarcerated; but for him it will mean that he is likely to find himself in a female juvenile detention centre and will have limited or no access to binding or packing materials.

## ACCESSING PUBLIC BATHROOMS

For most transgender young men, using public gendered bathrooms can be an anxiety-filled experience, as well as one that affirms their identity. Transgender men will often have the desire to use the male bathroom as it is more appropriate for them and doing so gives a sense of validation in their own gender identity. It can be an experience that is very positive and enabling for a young person or it can be an experience of terror, anxiety and violence.

Public bathrooms tend to have different social codes. For example, for women it is highly socially accepted to use them together in groups and for women to chat there with their friends. The men's bathroom is almost a completely different world. Men do not go to the bathroom in groups and chat to each other. Using the bathroom is not seen as sociable; it is a necessity, and that is how it is treated within male culture. The aim is to get in, do your business and leave. It is important that young people understand these differences in order to keep themselves safe.

When speaking to transgender men, they explain some of the thoughts they had before using the men's bathroom for the first time:

'I was nervous when I decided that I would use the men's bathroom for the first time. I didn't know whether I would receive abuse or not.' Anonymous

'I was nervous but really excited as well, I was hoping I wouldn't get misgendered and kicked out!' Anonymous

Transgender men have spoken of varying experiences of using public bathrooms, from absolute and total acceptance without any issues to violent assault and verbal abuse. One man explains that he had used the public bathrooms in an LGBT bar and had been verbally abused and pushed around in the toilets, the perpetrator stating that the man was in fact a lesbian and should not be in the men's toilets. The trans man explains that using public bathrooms is now an experience that fills him with anxiety rather than meeting his need to void his bladder in the right environment, which is how it used to be. He goes on to explain that prior to taking hormones he had his choice of bathrooms; he could have used the women's but chose to use the men's because he felt better in doing so and it alleviated gender dysphoria. He explains that when that incident happened, he had been taking testosterone for a year and there had been no incident prior to when he started hormone therapy, so he felt that there was still the potential for him to be misgendered, thus leading to anxiety. The man states that he felt the environment he was in (LGBT bar) should have been the most accepting place for him and should have been the safest place to use the bathrooms in peace because of the customers it caters to, so it was a shock to receive such a negative response from others in that bar.

The Equality Act 2010 states that a person who identifies as transgender has the right, under the act, to use the toilet/ changing facilities of their chosen expressed gender identity without fear or harassment. This applies to every organisation – those working with transgender young people, those who have transgender employees, schools, workplaces and even public buildings. There are things we can do to help support transgender people to use the bathroom that appropriately expresses their gender identity. It's important to remember that employers have to make 'reasonable adjustment' and that has to be justified, so to ask a service provider to knock down their building and construct a new one with gender neutral facilities will probably not be justified under 'making reasonable adjustment'. However, you can change the signs on the toilet doors to gender neutral ones, therefore making them accessible to not only binary transgender people and cisgender people but to also those that identify as being non-binary too.

School and college bathrooms are a complex issue. In this country we have split gender bathrooms and changing facilities and our schools teach different lessons to gender groups, for example physical education; that's how our country's education system operates, and to change that would be a huge challenge. So what can we do to support children and young people within the education system?

I'd like to note that some transgender men have been asked to use staff toilets, more specifically staff female toilets. This is highly inappropriate on a variety of levels. First and foremost, it is imperative that we have separate toilets for staff and young people in schools to create and maintain professional boundaries. It also helps to ensure that staff feel secure in using the bathroom and are not worried about accusations being made because schools will strictly adhere to the rules in terms of staff accessing staff bathrooms and pupils using theirs, which is equally important. Staff have the right to feel safe in using the bathrooms at work as much as transgender pupils, and employees have the right to use the bathroom of their choice freely and without fear of harassment.

School can be a difficult time for most teenagers, let alone if you identify as a transgender man. There are a few things we can do to help support someone in using the bathroom appropriate for them:

- Ask the young person what they would prefer to do. This will give you an idea of what their expectation is and how you can support them to do what they feel is best.

- Explore the possibility of giving young people 'bathroom passes' allowing them to leave class to use the bathroom. There are likely to be fewer people in the bathroom of their choice during lesson times. You may think, 'But they'll miss out on their lessons!' However, they'll be missing out on their lessons anyway if all they're thinking is that they're desperate for the toilet but can't use it, so a few minutes out of a lesson will encourage re-engagement when they come back into class.

- Consider having staff members to monitor bathroom use and challenge inappropriate behaviour from others if it is seen/heard.

- Make a toilet in your school gender neutral. It might seem a difficult thing to do; however, most of the time, all it takes is for the signs to be replaced on the doors, stating that they are gender neutral toilets.

- Can the same be done for changing facilities?

- Ensure that your school bullying policies and policies to support gender variant children and young people are up to date, and if you haven't got a policy relating to gender reassignment at school…make one. If you're reading this book because you're trying to support a gender variant/gender non-conforming young person, they could help you write that policy to help you to understand the needs of transgender men more. Engaging transgender people in policy writing is key to ensuring that you get a variety of perspectives so that you can address issues before they happen.

In terms of providing for service users, obviously the above list may not be appropriate; however, it does depend on what type of service you provide. For example, a service that provides supported accommodation to young people will have to make different changes to a service that provides a weekly youth club.

Think about the service you provide, and the things you can do to change your service to ensure that transgender people are safe and welcome to use your facilities. Brainstorm with your team and make sure that the young people you're supporting are at the heart of what you're proposing.

If you provide same sex accommodation, and a young transgender person wishes to be placed in a male flat with another male young person, it is up to them to decide whether or not their flat mate knows about them being transgender. They may find it easier to disclose this to their flat mate or they might not; it's in their hands. Of course, depending on their decision, you will have to manage the process with other young people involved to ensure that their voices, opinions and considerations are taken into account and that all young people you support are happy with any decisions the staff team make.

## BULLYING AND HATE CRIME

Bullying is a common experience for trans people, especially young people. Bullying is common in educational settings and within local communities and is often not taken seriously and seen as 'kids just being kids'. However, bullying damages young people's mental health, self-esteem and confidence and can lead to young people committing suicide. If bullying is not taken seriously in schools and institutions, young people will never feel safe and free from harm, and all young people have the right to that. As professionals, we must take allegations of bullying seriously. Check your school's/project's bullying policies. Are they clear and concise? Are they easy to follow? Many schools have a zero tolerance attitude to bullying; however, just 'telling off a young person' who has bullied another can make things worse. Be creative with challenging bullying. Be strict on bullying policies; zero tolerance means zero tolerance. If young people are bullying others because they are transgender, this is a hate crime and can be reported to the police, so it needs to be taken seriously by institutions. Suspension from school usually follows a serious incident. Treat transphobic behaviour as a serious incident and make sure that young people can feel safe and confident in coming to you to report transphobia. Encouraging an environment where everyone is equal and deserves equal respect and can learn in a safe environment is the best possible way to get the right outcomes for young people. This can't be compromised for one person because they are different from others; they have those rights too and these should be upheld by institutions. Have a strict anti-bullying policy. Invite local LGBT services to come and run a session with staff or young people or both about how they can challenge transphobic behaviour within school in ways that are effective and not tokenistic. Use the strategies that have been learned through these sessions to build a strict anti-bullying policy that will be followed when bullying is reported. Transphobia needs to be taken seriously at all levels. Whether it's being reported by young people or adults, it is a criminal offence and people can be prosecuted for transphobic actions and behaviours.

Unfortunately hate crime is still a part of everyday life for transgender people. Hate crime is a crime and should be treated as such. It is a serious offence under the Equality Act (2010), and sentencing guidelines are used from the Criminal Justice Act (2003) to convict perpetrators of hate crime. Hate crime towards transgender people increased by 170 per cent in 2016 (Yeung 2016). Transphobia is a serious offence that many transgender people struggle with on a daily basis and one that causes serious harm to mental health and emotional wellbeing.

Transphobia can take a variety of forms from verbal and emotional abuse, to physical assault, sexual assault, name calling, vandalism to property, discrimination within the workplace, online bullying and harassment.

Some transgender people report that they are fearful of leaving their house, their house is vandalised on a regular basis by people who live in their local communities and some have written transphobic slurs on their properties. Transgender people are degraded, humiliated and verbally and physically abused – sometimes on a regular basis – because they are trans. This sort of trauma can lead to social isolation and a very fast decline in mental health. For someone who cannot leave their home through fear of threats and violence, this can lead into a debilitating depression. Lack of understanding and acceptance within local communities can lead to transgender people committing suicide. People have to feel safe where they live, and if they have not got that support or safety within their own home and in their communities, they may feel that they will struggle to find it elsewhere if they can't leave the house. They may turn to the internet for support and start engaging with chat rooms to seek acceptance and support. This can in some cases be beneficial for young people; however, it can also put them at significant risk if they are engaging with people online who they do not know and who may have ulterior motives for wanting to build a trusting relationship with them.

Transphobia has serious consequences for those who are its victims. Transgender people have been beaten in the streets, and in more serious cases murdered. In the United States, 48 out of 50 states still have a clause called 'Trans Panic', which means that if the defendant claims they were in a state of panic because of someone's gender identity, they can use lethal force and not be prosecuted for doing so (The LGBT Bar 2017).

It is crucial that young people are aware of their rights as transgender men. They need to understand what constitutes a hate crime and what can be reported to the police. Informal sessions around trans rights and hate crime are a good way to introduce what young people are entitled to in this country and to educate about what they can expect in terms of police protection from hate crime.

It is our duty to encourage young people to report hate crime wherever possible. This can be difficult for a young person, especially for someone who has suffered a serious and traumatic hate crime. It is likely their mental health will suffer as a consequence and they will experience high levels of anxiety and increased bouts of depression. All perpetrators of hate crime should be brought to justice, and no transgender person should suffer because of someone else's ignorance.

If a young person is worried about what will happen once their report has been received by the police, professionals can enlist the support of their local police community support officer (PCSO), who may be able to attend your project/service to talk to the young person in confidence prior to making a complaint to the police. This way they can understand the process of what will happen once the report has been received, therefore putting their mind at ease.

If a young person does not wish to report the crime to the police, encourage them to take photographs of any injuries they have sustained and write down what happened as soon as possible after the incident. Reassure them that their information and photographs of injuries will be kept securely in case they change their mind at a later date. It is important that if a young person does wish to proceed with a complaint to the police any evidence is preserved and their memory of the event is not compromised with time. Write down any specific details of the perpetrators that the young person can remember. If the young person is under the age of 16, it is advisable that you speak with your local children's safeguarding board with regards to their policy on reporting hate crimes for those under 16. Transgender people over the age of 18 have a choice as to whether or not to report hate crimes that they may have suffered, and this choice must remain with them.

A multi-agency approach to safeguarding young people from hate crime will foster young people's safety and will ensure that they obtain the best possible support from agencies around them. You can enlist support from the following agencies for a multi-agency strategy:

- Victim Support

- Sexual Assault Referral Centres (SARCs)

- hate crime reporting centres

- Citizens Advice Bureaus

- local housing officers/neighbourhood officers/support workers from housing associations

- the Albert Kennedy Trust – provides support for those living in a hostile environment or made homeless who are LGBT

- local PCSOs and police officers

- children's services.

Ensure you have the young person's consent (if appropriate) as to whether or not to engage these services. If each service works together to create a strategy to protect the service user from harm, the better and more positive the outcome for the young person will be.

# Chapter 4

# SOCIAL TRANSITION LOGISTICS

We need to remember that not everyone will want to take steps towards social transition; some are just happy presenting to the world as male in a stereotypical sense, while some will want to change their names officially, obtain ID in their new names and so on. In this chapter we'll look at how each of the different logistical elements of social transition come together and how they can be obtained by young people with your support.

## CHANGING NAMES

In order for young people to have the legal right to change their names on official documentation such as the school register or to obtain ID in their new names, they will have to have legally changed their name. There are two options in order to do this: the deed poll (free or paid for) or the statutory declaration.

The deed poll is the easiest option in my opinion; there's a free deed poll available online and there's also the enrolled version. The free deed poll service is a legitimate and legal way to change someone's name; it is just as official as receiving a deed poll through a solicitor. However, this is only available to young people aged 16 and above.

The government website[1] explains that you can write your own deed poll and you don't need any additional public or private bodies to do this. It explains that in order to do this you must state the following as an example of writing your own deed poll:

'I [old name] of [your address] have given up my name [old name] and have adopted for all purposes the name [new name].'

'Signed as a deed on [date] as [old name] and [new name] in the presence of [witness 1 name] of [witness 1 address], and [witness 2 name] of [witness 2 address].'

'[your new signature], [your old signature]'

'[witness 1 signature], [witness 2 signature]'

The government currently recommends that you 'enrol' your deed poll with the Royal Court of Justice. There is a charge to this, and this refers to your deed poll being kept in the Royal Court of Justice for five to ten years and then being moved to the National Archives. Enrolling a deed poll does not make the deed poll more official in nature; it solely refers to making a permanent name change public. In order to enrol a deed poll you must be aged 18 years or over.

Young people will need to consider whether or not to enrol their deed poll, and in order to make this decision they need to find out whether organisations that they plan on changing their name with will accept a deed poll that is not enrolled; they just need to ask the question at the bank and so on.

I have a free deed poll that I obtained from the internet. You input your details (as per the template above), find some fancy paper and print it off, get your witnesses to sign it and submit the original to organisations for changing your name. I changed my name at every organisation to my new name without issue.

---

1    https://www.gov.uk/change-name-deed-poll

No one questioned it; no one required an enrolled deed poll in order for me to obtain a passport in my new name, a driving licence in my new name or to change my name at the bank, on the electoral roll, with DVLA for my vehicles, my student loan accounts and so on. It's worth obtaining a free deed poll first before paying for it, because at least that way young people may save themselves some money.

Young people can also obtain a statutory declaration through a solicitors firm in order to change their name. This service carries a price which varies from solicitor to solicitor, and the only known benefit is that if a solicitor does carry out this service it appears more 'official' and the young person is less likely to run into any issues when changing their names with relevant organisations. It's worth shopping around for quotes to obtain the statutory declaration if that's what a young person chooses to do; however, it's worth trying the free online deed poll services first as the young person could save themselves a few hundred pounds!

If children/young people under the age of 16 wish to change their name officially, then there is a different process to consider, one which will require a few documents first in order to achieve an official and legal deed poll.

They first need to obtain parental permission from those who care for them, and all parties who hold parental responsibility need to agree to the name change. If the child has a caregiver/foster carer or is looked after by social services, then whoever is responsible for the child will need to be in agreement before obtaining a deed poll. It may be that social services need to obtain parental permission anyway, dependent on which sections of law a child in care is under. Failing an attempt to reach an agreement, a young person is allowed to file for a court order to change their name. It is best if an agreement by all parties can be sought first, as obtaining a court order will incur charges and a significant amount of stress on relationships. It currently costs £215 to change a child's name by court order and £36 if all parties are in agreement with the name change, so it needs to be considered carefully and the options weighed up first.

It's important that all accounts held by the young person are changed in order to ensure there is no confusion if accounts are linked; for example, if someone changed their name with HMRC but not their employer, it may bring up some issues! You'll need to consider the following places to present a deed poll (not an exhaustive list). Note that some organisations may incur a charge for this service:

- GP, dentist, opticians

- DVLA (charge), DLA, DWP, Passport Office (charge), Inland Revenue, Council Tax, ATOS

- school, college, university, Student Finance

- for trans parents: schools, clubs, education department, free school meals, uniform, nursery, specialists, support, social services, Department for Transport, carers agencies, respite, grant, child care, nappy services and family fund

- pay roll/pension providers

- utilities companies, bank account, credit card accounts, credit reference agencies, landlord (if renting), housing association, insurance companies, TV licensing, broadband provider, telephone/mobile provider

- library cards, loyalty cards, rail cards, travel cards, Oyster cards, gym membership

- social services, specialists, support groups, Department for Transport, carer agency

- for those who have children with special needs: social services, respite care services, SEN department.

It will be useful for a transgender person to make a list of all agencies they feel they need to change their name at. It can be an extensive list, so writing it down and ticking items off as and when they are complete will help, as it can be stressful and exhausting having to repeat yourself so many times to so many different people. It's important to take a break and remember it doesn't all have to be done in a couple of hours. Prioritise the most important things first, or alternatively, if a young person is feeling anxious about changing their name, maybe try changing it on a rail card first or similar service before approaching the DVLA or Passport Office.

It is important to note that offices such as the DVLA and Passport Office will require additional evidence to be submitted when applying for a change in driving licence/passport. For the Passport Office the young person will need *one* of the following in addition to their deed poll:

- a birth or adoption certificate in their acquired gender

- a gender recognition certificate

- a letter from their GP/medical consultant confirming that their change of gender is to be permanent

- evidence of using their new name such as a bank statement or medical letter.

If young people have dual nationality or a non-UK passport, they will have to submit travel documents/residency permits alongside the above. The Home Office policy does make an exception for transgender people who originate from countries where changing your gender on passports is illegal and will endeavour to support young people who wish to have their UK documentation in their new name.

Note that changes in legislation and the Gender Recognition Act may be reformed over the years and therefore may affect the criteria required for people to change their names and gender on official documentation such as passports and driving licences. Information on these changes are usually available at the government website.

## OBTAINING A GENDER RECOGNITION CERTIFICATE

A gender recognition certificate (GRC) is, in essence, the document which replaces someone's original birth certificate. It can be useful for a variety of different reasons for a trans person to have one. For example, in any situation that requires the young person to submit their birth certificate, such as getting married, the GRC would be submitted instead. Therefore a young person is legally recognised as a man. In most situations, there are conflicting guidelines between government organisations; for example, you can obtain a passport without having a GRC, but you have to get married using your birth certificate if you don't have a GRC, and that would change the essence of the relationship in the eyes of the law. So a trans man without a GRC getting married to a cisgender woman would be seen as a gay marriage in the eyes of the law because of the need to submit a birth certificate for the ceremony.

Many people choose not to obtain a GRC because for the most part transgender people don't need one in the same way as they need a passport, for example. It generally tends to impact on changing gender with HMRC and getting married.

In order to obtain a GRC to replace a birth certificate, the young person will need to fill out the relevant application form depending on their circumstances, which can be found on the government website (see the Additional Information section for details). The young person will have to choose which application they fill in depending on whether they are single, married or in a civil partnership. The application is different for those who are married or in a civil partnership because their partner has to give their written permission and submit this to the GRC board as evidence that they are happy their partner will be seen in the eyes of the law as a man, therefore possibly changing the status of their marriage.

Evidence for applications varies depending on which application a young person fills out; however, young people will need to submit the following:

- original or certified copy of birth certificate

- copies of any official documents that show birth name has changed to current name

- proof they have lived in their acquired gender for the required time (two years)

- any medical reports

- passport

- driving licence

- payslips or benefit documents

- utility bills or other documents of an official nature.

All documents should be in the acquired name and gender and the earliest document must be dated before the beginning of the required time (at least two years prior to submitting an application).

The young person will then submit this evidence to the gender panel along with £140 for the application fee. Young people who are eligible can claim this money back if they are on certain benefits or a low income.

The panel will discuss whether or not the person has done enough to obtain a GRC and will either grant one or not based on the information provided.

Generally, the panel tends to grant GRCs after a young person has had top surgery; however, it is not unheard of for the panel to grant the certificate prior to that if the young person provides enough evidence and a supporting letter if they have chosen not to have top surgery. Gender clinics often advise patients to apply for a GRC after top surgery. Trans men have to submit a variety of evidence in order for the panel to accept their application, and are asked where in their physical transition they currently are. The panel is unlikely to accept an application for a GRC prior to top surgery because legally changing a person's gender will impact on things like pensions, so the panel needs to be absolutely certain the change in gender will be permanent, which is more likely to happen if a young person has had top surgery. As the application costs a significant amount of cash, it's important that young people applying for a GRC do not get rejected, as this will cost them more money in the future. However, top surgery is not necessary in order to apply for a GRC, and whether it is appropriate must be assessed on an individual basis, considering the young person's best interests and the timing of their transition.

## PASSING

Passing, by definition and as touched upon in previous chapters, is the concept whereby a young person presents in their male role (usually stereotypically) in order to ensure that other people such as the general public refer to them as male when they go out into the world. Often people will subtly inform young people whether or not they think they are presenting as male and female through a variety of different ways, the most common of which is language. As a society we have certain terms of endearment that we will use with people of different genders; for example, a woman may be referred to as love or sweetheart, and a man is usually referred to as mate, buddy and so on. It wouldn't be usual to come across a man who refers to another man as love or sweetheart and vice versa for women. These terms will subtly inform children and young people whether or not they have 'passed' in public, and this can be a cause of great stress and anxiety. If young people feel that they are unable to pass in public, it can lead to social isolation and anxiety, encouraging young people to withdraw from society and stay in their own safe spaces, therefore affecting social development.

As discussed earlier, the whole concept of passing in itself is one that has to be questioned; transgender young people should not need to 'pass' in order to obtain the gender affirmation that they require. People should not be judged based on their appearance and should be given the opportunity to inform others of their gender before they are misgendered or before judgements are made on their gender in the first place. However, as I'm sure we can agree, that is very idealistic, so the topic of passing is important to transgender young people in order to decrease the dysphoria they feel.

To reiterate a point made earlier, it is important that we remember to encourage individuality and comfort for young people and teach them to be powerful in their own sense of gender identity regardless of how the world reacts to them. This will promote positive self-esteem and confidence in appropriately and confidently challenging those people who may question or challenge their identities.

Masculinity is different for everyone; what makes one person feel masculine may not create the same feeling for others, so it's important that young people are given the opportunity to explore what makes them feel at their best. This can be binding, packing, clothing or just being themselves!

Trans men who have been through the process of social transition have shared how they feel about passing and what's important. The key thing that was evident and consistent was that young people need to be confident. Trans men shared:

'Be confident in your gender expression and identity; even if you're shaking inside, go out into the world and project yourself as a man, challenge people if you are misgendered, make a joke out of it if you have to but be confident in doing so because that will make the difference. There are many ways of being a man in modern society, so don't be afraid to be yourself, be feminine, androgynous or stereotypically masculine, do whatever feels comfortable and right for you; the most important thing is that you feel that you are projecting the image of yourself to the world that you see yourself when you look in the mirror.' Anonymous

It can be reassuring for young people to spend time with other men in order to develop an understanding of what they might expect when socialising with men. This may help them to develop their own sense of identity, and if passing is important to them, understanding and learning about male culture may aid passing in general.

The following sections will try to deliver an understanding of what transgender men may do in order to reduce dysphoria and the chances of being misgendered. It is my belief that misgendering happens when others use stereotypes to determine gender, and therefore respond the way they think they should. Often people use physical cues if they are unsure of a person's gender, so they will look at clothing or someone's chest to determine whether or not they have breasts, for example, or at people's crotches to determine whether or not there is evidence of a bulge-like shape. Transgender men often try to reduce misgendering by using methods that create masculine features; this can lead to less misgendering, which ultimately supports gender affirmation and positive mental health.

## Binding

Binding is a common method used by transgender people in order to reduce dysphoria. Many transgender men bind and some choose not to; again, it is a young person's choice as to whether or not they bind. Binding is the method used to flatten breast tissue to create a chest with a more masculine appearance. Men have flat chests; the point of binding is to induce that flat chest for transgender men in order to reduce dysphoria and aid passing in society.

There are many different methods of binding. One of the most appropriate and safest ways is to buy a binder from a credible company. A binder is a compression vest, which is usually made from a combination of medical grade nylon and spandex and is shaped as a vest. The binder usually has a double panel front and a single at the back in order to provide the additional compression at the front.

Binding can be a painful experience and it is advised that people wear their binders for no more than eight hours per day continuously and where possible regularly take breaks from binding. It is important that young transgender men are advised not to sleep in their binders. Binding causes breathing restriction due to the intense compression of the chest, so sleeping in a binder can be very dangerous.

Binding can cause health issues, and young people need to be aware of some of the complications that can arise. It's important that as professionals we advise young people to listen to their bodies and take positive action if side effects start to occur. If a young person gets a cold, it is advisable not to bind during this time; coughing will exacerbate injuries and cause further injury to a young person's body if binding with a cold. Many people will go to work and school when they have a cold; however, for a transgender man who has to bind and still attend school/work with a cold, this can be a really challenging thing to do because of the pain they will experience. Coughing while binding is particularly dangerous because the lungs expand when coughing and the ribs are pushed against the binder as a consequence. This can lead to serious injury, so it's advisable for young people to stay home and desist from binding when they have a cold/cough. Young people will heal faster than they would if they just carried on. In a study recently conducted by the Binding Health Project at Boston University (Peitzmeier 2015), they found the most common problems associated with binding are:

- shortness of breath

- pain: breast pain and back and rib pain

- fractured ribs

- bruising

- aching.

Many transgender men experience side effects as described above when they bind for too long. Purpose-made binders can be expensive depending on the models and choices that are picked. It is common for young people to search the internet for alternative methods of binding if they cannot afford to buy a binder that is made specifically for that purpose.

One of the biggest impacts on the human body that binding can have is that breast tissue will change with prolonged use of a binder. Breasts will change in their appearance; they will potentially appear flatter because, as binding occurs, the breast tissue is generally pushed downwards, therefore giving the illusion of a flatter chest, but this has dramatic consequences in terms of aesthetics. This will likely not be an issue for trans men who are secure in their identity and plan on having surgery. However, if someone does bind long term and decides it is no longer of use for them, it's important to recognise that binding will change breast tissue over a significant period of time and that it does not recover from this. Young people need to take this into consideration when they are deciding whether or not they wish to bind their chests.

Most websites offering binders that are made specifically for compression of the chest will have a size chart so that young people can find the right-sized binder for them. It is often tempting for young people to find the right size of binder and then buy one size smaller because of the assumption that, if you get a smaller binder, your chest will appear flatter. This is not the case; if young people do buy binders that are too small for them, the chance of them experiencing injuries and discomfort is greater. It is important that young people choose the right-sized binder for their chest size. Websites also offer diagrams and explanations of how people should measure themselves in order to find the right binder for them.

Young people will also come across the following methods if they search the internet:

- binding with duct tape

- binding with cling film

- binding with masking tape

- double binding (two compression vests)

- binding with sports bras

- binding by wearing multiple tight-fitting t-shirts and/ or jumpers.

These are dangerous methods of binding and cause multiple issues. When trans young people use these methods, it is highly likely that they will not understand how tight to bind, so in order to obtain a completely flat chest, they will often bind too tightly, which restricts breathing. This can lead to a young person losing consciousness and increases the risks of the above-mentioned complications occurring. Most men do not have a completely flat chest, and it is important that this is reiterated to young people in order to educate on binding and masculine-looking chests. Every man is different.

It is advised that young people obtain a binder from a credible source and not try to bind themselves using the above methods. This will ensure that young people's bodies remain as healthy as possible but their need to reduce gender dysphoria and pass in society is still met. This is the best way to ensure optimal physical and mental health.

If young people are struggling to afford a binder, research your local LGBT support networks. There are many charities that offer a binder service whereby people will donate their old binders after having top surgery and these are then offered to others for free or for a small donation. Also consider whether or not your service could provide financial support for a young person to obtain a binder. The outcome of doing so will be increased emotional health and wellbeing due to a reduction in dysphoria and will also encourage safe binding methods.

When the weather gets hotter, binding will become more difficult for a young person. Generally, the bigger chest a young person has, the more inclined they will be to double bind and wear a t-shirt rather than use a single binder and wear a jumper. Both options come with their own difficulties, especially when the weather is hot. Binding will become uncomfortable, cause rashes of the skin from sweating due to not being dressed appropriately for the weather, and dehydration will occur a lot faster. Encourage young people to always single bind and wear t-shirts that are a size too big; this will help alleviate sweating, thus reducing the risks of skin rashes and dehydration while maintaining a reduced level of gender dysphoria. Encourage young people to drink water regularly. If they collapse because they are dehydrated they will no doubt be admitted to hospital and will need to be cut free from their binders. This can be a traumatic experience and one that is best avoided if young people are encouraged to look after themselves and take positive steps towards promoting their physical health.

The type of service you provide will affect what you can realistically provide for young people who are struggling with binding. If you're a school, perhaps young people can be given bathroom passes to use the bathrooms/changing rooms for a short period of time for some privacy to take their binder off during the day for a break. Can you provide a bathroom at your service that offers enough privacy for a young person to use it to take their binder off for short periods of time and ensure they won't be disturbed while having a break from binding?

Ask your service user what would be most beneficial to them. They may feel that they don't need support in ensuring that they get a break from binding and are fine; others may have their own suggestions.

Always advise young people to have a rest day from binding, when they can stay at home or at a safe place. Can your service provide a safe enough space for young people to take a break from binding while they are working with you? You will of course need to ensure that other service users/professionals do not make inappropriate comments towards young people and that you provide a safe enough space for young people to feel confident enough to do this. The chances of young people leaving the house without their binder is very small indeed; however, by being able to provide that space or at least offer it, you'll be sending the message that it is OK to be transgender and that young people will be accepted and supported at your service regardless of their presentation.

For a young person who is in employment and is finding binding at work difficult, if their employer is aware of their trans status then it may be worth having a conversation with them. If their employer is supportive of their transition, then they will no doubt try to accommodate and support the young person as best they can by making reasonable adjustments.

The industry the young person works in will determine what reasonable adjustments can be made. Consider the following:

- The young person should be encouraged to take their breaks! They should resist the temptation to work through them, which often happens with young workers.

- If the workplace is close to home, could the young person go home during their breaks and take a break from binding?

- Could breaks be split up throughout the day?

- Can a young person use the bathrooms/changing facilities in private at key intervals in order to have a break from binding?

- Can fans be made available in hotter weather, especially if working indoors?

- Are window restrictors causing problems in hotter weather? Can they be released at key times to air the office and ensure staff, especially trans men, remain cooler?

Again, the young person knows their workplace and manager better than anyone else, so they may have their own suggestions. If the young person lives their life as a stealth trans person, then it's important that emphasis is put on what they can do themselves that will help them to recover from the impacts of binding more quickly, because they will not necessarily feel that they can reach out for support because they wish for their trans status to remain unknown.

When people are stressed their bodies take longer to heal from injuries, so stress management is a key part of ensuring that physical and mental health are managed positively. If young people are stressed and are binding for significant lengths of time, then they will be more likely to sustain injuries from binding and to be unable to recover from those injuries, thus making it near impossible to continue binding without needing time off work. Everything has a knock-on effect. If a young person is stressed and injured from binding but can't take time off school/college/work to recover from those injuries, and having breaks from binding during the day has not been made a possibility, then the impact can be significant. Mental health will start to deteriorate; no one likes being in pain. Young people will not perform at their best wherever they are, be it education or employment; stress levels will continue to increase and it will become harder and harder to achieve what they need to on a day-to-day basis and to face the day. The more stress people's bodies are put under, then the more likely they are to sustain more serious injuries such as fractured ribs and the more time it will take to recover from injuries. If this happens, young people will need time off sick from their obligations, thus impacting on education or employment, which can affect their career and could lead to being dismissed if they have too much time off sick. If young people are struggling with injuries from binding, it is likely that they will try to meet their obligations to education/work and then go home and stay at home instead of engaging in activities that promote positive mental health, such as meeting up with friends, thus resulting in a vicious circle.

Exercise is known to promote positive physical and mental health; however, exercising in a binder is very difficult and as discussed earlier restricts breathing, so engaging in exercise while binding can do more damage than good. Exercise releases endorphins that relieve stress and promote good mental health and emotional wellbeing, so encourage young people to go for a walk in their breaks or conduct other forms of gentle exercise. If they feel confident in exercising without binding then encourage that as much as possible. Sports bras offer a limited amount of compression but can be a good solution to exercising without binding. Walking, yoga and even walking football are all good examples of gentle exercise that will promote good mental and physical wellbeing.

It's important that as professionals working with young people we try to highlight potential consequences of actions in order to ensure that young people have as much information as possible for making an informed choice about how they manage their overall health.

Consider what may happen if a young person overuses their binder and loses consciousness at school/college/work. The most appropriate course of action would be to call an ambulance or take them to hospital to get checked out. If that happens, they will have to face more professionals and explain what has happened, which may cause discomfort and embarrassment especially if the professionals that a young person encounters at A&E have limited knowledge on trans health issues. If they are unconscious as a direct result of binding and are tended to by paramedics they may cut their binder off, and again a young person would have to deal with being in a public place without their binder and the paramedics' responses after it's happened.

Discomfort and embarrassment in front of others affect our mental health and self-esteem. It's important that young people consider all possible outcomes of their actions and therefore make decisions that are right for them, knowing the full consequences.

We must promote positive actions for health for every transgender man that we are working with. We need to encourage young people to take responsibility for their actions and their health.

The following are some top tips to pass onto the young trans person to promote positive wellbeing while binding:

- Use a binder that is made specifically for binding.

- Choose the binder that is the correct size for you.

- Choose a t-shirt a size too big when the weather is hot.
- Concentrate on being sufficiently hydrated.
- Take breaks from binding where possible.
- Never bind for more than eight hours continuously.
- Never sleep in a binder.
- Never double bind.
- Socialise with friends to stay connected and stress-free.
- Take up a new hobby to relieve stress outside of day-to-day obligations.
- Take up gentle exercise.

## Packing

Packing is the term used to describe a method of dysphoria reduction by creating the image that someone has a penis. Clothing that men wear allows for space in the front for their penis, so when transgender men wear men's clothes without packing it can cause the area to look flat and may lead to people being misgendered because of other people's assessments of gender in its stereotypical form. For many transgender men, packing helps to reduce dysphoria by making them feel that they have a penis and therefore ensures that they feel more aligned with their gender identity.

There are many different types of packing; the most common is for transgender men to use a specific packer, designed for its purpose. In its basic form it is a silicone penis that is worn in the underwear to create the impression of a penis.

The specification of packers will determine how much people spend. There are packers that are very basic such as the one discussed already (silicone flaccid penis), and at the more expensive end of the scale, it is possible to buy packers that can be used for sex, masturbation, urinating and packing. A standard silicone packer can be bought for approximately £15. For the higher spec models people can pay up to £200.

Packing is different for everyone, and what people want to get from their packers will help them decide which one to buy. In my personal experience, the standard packer works very well; it's quite difficult to use the high specification models because they are very bulky and using them as a packer on their own creates quite an offensive-looking image. However, this is generally the case with men who are short. It takes a lot of practice to be able to use the high specification models for their purposes, and if people can afford to buy different ones with different specifications I would encourage them to do so to find what's right for them.

Many transgender young men will experiment with standing up to pee. You can buy 'STP' (stand to pee) packers to enable this. Most of the cheaper STP packers use the standard silicone penis model with a hollowed-out centre and plastic insert shaped in a similar way to the 'Shewee'. This allows people to use public bathrooms using the STP function, reducing dysphoria and contributing to their ability to pass. It can be a very affirming thing to use STP products as it makes transgender men feel they have what they should have had in the beginning.

It can be difficult to use the STP function on packers. It takes a lot of practice, and it is advisable that you suggest your service users practise before using one in public. Many transgender people will practise in the shower, which can help them get used to their bodies and understand what to expect from their packer. Patience is key, and getting it right takes time. It's important not to rush out and use a public bathroom after the first successful attempt, because the chances of accidents happening are quite high. If transgender men do use their STP in public bathrooms, it is important that they are aware that if they are not confident in doing so it is likely they will have an accident and end up with pee all down their legs and clothes, which would of course be very embarrassing and traumatic for a transgender man. Some people use the STP functions and others don't, preferring to pee as they usually would, and that's OK; it doesn't make people any less trans to do so.

It is important to recognise that if people do use a packer then there are things they will need to do to care for it in order to prolong its use. If packers are bought specifically from companies that create them for trans people, then they will usually come with care guidelines. Most of the lower spec packers don't have these. People will find, with the cheaper flaccid packers, that the silicone is sticky and can irritate the skin, so many transgender men coat them in cornflour in order to reduce the sticky feeling; this also protects the packer. Most of the higher grade packers do not require the use of cornflour, but the majority of silicone packers do.

We must advise young people to wash their packers regularly! It is important as they will become discoloured from underwear and use in general and the silicone will degrade. Once they have been washed they will return to feeling sticky, so the cornflour should be used again. Some people just buy a new one once they feel they need to, and that's OK if they can afford it, but if they can't, caring for their packer is an important consideration.

Packers that are used to urinate with should be washed after every use. It can be difficult for young people who are using them to urinate in public bathrooms to just get them out and give them a wash! So consider advising a young person to keep wet wipes with them and use the cubicle. If young people would rather use the urinal they should ensure that the packer is at least washed daily and remember to make sure all urine is out of the packer before putting it away or else it will end up leaking, which again can be a cause of embarrassment.

Some transgender men use medical grade adhesive to attach their packer to their skin. I would urge that people only do this if they are absolutely certain it is what they want. If medical grade adhesive is used and there is a problem with the packer while you're out and about, then you're going to have issues in removing it safely. Medical grade adhesives for packers are sold specifically for that purpose; don't use normal glue! They are sold with the adhesive remover also. The adhesives are designed for all-day hold, so people need to be sure that this is something they want to do before they do it! It can cause skin irritation, and if you're using your packer to STP, and using medical adhesive, and find that the packer moves or isn't in the right position, getting it off is going to be an issue in a public place.

Transgender people use varying ways to secure their packers: some just use tighter boxers and the packer sits in them, with some movement and adjustment needed throughout the day; others use specific packer holders worn below their hips, which ensures that less movement and adjustment is needed throughout the day; and others use medical adhesive. Some people design their own packer holders and have sewn additional pockets into their boxers, creating a more secure way to wear their packer.

It's also important to consider that young people who are on a low income may not have the funds to buy a specific packer. Unlike binding, people can pack with most items you'd find in your house. The most comfortable options are rolled-up socks; this still creates the bulge that people want and creates the feeling that they have a penis.

Be sure to advise young people not to use any items that are going to irritate skin or be uncomfortable, as this will just cause problems throughout the day. If a young person is packing with something that does make them feel uncomfortable, then the chances are that's what they'll be thinking about instead of engaging with their school lessons or concentrating on work.

It is also important to consider the activities that will be undertaken when deciding on the most appropriate packer and holding method. Having tighter boxers to hold the packer and nothing else to secure it will be no use for an activity that involves a lot of body movements such as dancing or football. There would be a significant amount of explaining to do if a packer flew out of the bottom of someone's trouser leg because it wasn't secured properly! Again, the impact this will have on a young person's self-esteem and confidence would be considerable, especially if it happened in a place like school or college.

## Clothing

Clothing can be a major anxiety-inducing experience; it can also be very validating for a young person. Shopping for the first time for men's clothes may be quite a daunting experience but can be exciting too!

It's important that we make sure young people are as informed as possible before they take a shopping trip so that they understand what they might be walking into and have strategies to deal with potential issues along the way.

Men's clothes sizes are different to women's. If young people don't understand the difference between the clothing sizes, then it may be beneficial to conduct an informal session around this so that they understand what they are looking for.

Men's clothes are tailored for men's bodies; they don't take into account transgender men's. For example, men's bodies generally do not have hips that protrude, and clothes on the high street will reflect this. Young people need to be aware of this because if they choose something based on the size they think they are by comparing women's sizes to men's, then enter the changing rooms to find that their hips stick out or the item doesn't sit right on their chest, this can be very daunting and disappointing for them. They may decide to give up trying to buy men's clothes because of what's happened. Some young people will reconsider their transition at points when they are embarrassed or upset about things that have happened such as in this scenario. There's nothing wrong with re-evaluating at key points of transition; however, it's important that we see such negative experiences as an external one and one that possibly could have been prevented given the right advice and information. It may be better for young people to choose clothing that is one size too big as this will not exaggerate features as much, thus leading to feeling affirmed in their gender. Young people can then enjoy the way they feel when wearing men's clothes and the image portrayed back to them in the mirror. This may be the first time that they feel aligned with their gender identity; it should be a positive and validating experience. Knowledge is power in these situations.

Encourage the young person to consider choosing men's specific clothing stores. These tend to have 'changing rooms' rather than men's changing rooms and women's changing rooms. It will be more difficult for retail staff to stop a young person from entering a changing room that is gender neutral as opposed to one that is gender specific. It is worth considering which shops a young person wishes to visit and researching whether or not the shops have gender-specific changing facilities. You can find most information online, but if you struggle, a call to the shop will soon give clarification.

It can be a very disheartening experience for a young person who goes shopping to finally pick the clothes they want to try on and then get told at the changing rooms which ones to use. Most cisgender people take this for granted. You get into the changing rooms and the staff tell you to either go left or right, based on the gender identity that they have chosen for you. It sounds absurd in itself and it is. For a cisgender person it will be completely normal, but if a retail staff member misgenders a transgender young person and they end up using the changing facilities that are not right for them, it can be a truly devastating and embarrassing experience. If staff leave it up to young people to choose for themselves and don't challenge them, or if they point them in the direction of the 'right' changing rooms, it will be a completely different experience. It's a gamble for young people, especially those who are not confident in challenging people when they are misgendered. The more a young person is misgendered, the more they will feel negative about themselves, thus impacting on self-esteem. It could in fact lead young people to get into debt by using catalogue services instead.

Some people use catalogues and manage their debt, but for a young person who is on a low income, this can be a great way for them to buy the things that they want, try the clothes on in a safe environment but then continue to buy clothes, which ultimately will be a positive experience but comes with all the stresses and strains that debt involves, thus impacting on stress levels and overall mental health. If a young person does choose this method to buy their clothes, it's important that we provide them with appropriate money management skills in order to manage the debt they are accruing and budget appropriately. We need to advise on the consequences of not doing so.

The most important thing to remember when young people are buying new clothes is that they buy clothes that make them feel good; if they don't make them feel good then there will be no gender affirmation and they won't experience those positive feelings. Clothes are also a safe way to experience life as a man, projecting their image as a man to the world and experiencing how it feels to be transgender. It may bring up new feelings to explore and it may help young people to understand their identity more. If young people feel uncomfortable in their gender presentation once they've changed it, then that's OK, and it's all a part of growing and developing a sense of identity. It's also an easy fix if young people don't feel right in their gender expression. Clothes can be changed, but there's no going back from the impact of hormone therapy or surgery.

Some trans men share their experiences of using changing rooms:

'I've found that I am less likely to get challenged when I use men's specific clothing shops; I think people are more open minded now to women wearing men's clothes and so that concept in itself makes people less likely to challenge me. I'm not saying that what they see is a woman trying on men's clothes, it's just an added bonus so to speak. I'd rather be not challenged in a men's specific clothing shop than challenged and embarrassed in gender-specific ones.' Anonymous

'I have been challenged a few times in gender-specific changing rooms; once I got to the front of the queue to be told the women's changing rooms were on the right and the woman had pointed me in that direction. I felt hurt and embarrassed and I went in anyway, all the while feeling that I shouldn't be in there, but the thought of challenging someone in front of a huge queue of people was just too much for me. I'd had instead, [having] not tried on the clothes, stayed in the changing rooms on my phone for the amount of time that I thought would be normal enough before I could leave, leaving without the clothes I wanted to try on and leaving the shop completely. I've since felt nervous and anxious when trying on clothes and am reluctant to go shopping all together.' Anonymous

Most trans men that participated in the focus group state that confidence is key, as it is to a lot of elements of passing. If you're confident and you challenge someone, nine times out of ten you'll get an apology and an affirmation that states you can do what you see best, for example use the changing rooms of your choice. Most people who get challenged by transgender people are very embarrassed by what has happened and try to rectify the situation as quickly as possible in order to cause no further embarrassment to themselves.

To conclude, confidence is key, expectations should be discussed before a young person goes shopping and it's important to provide as much information as possible to them and empower them to challenge others. Consider a realistic solution to being misgendered. Think about words that the young person could use to challenge others, but ones that are appropriate for the situation. It's no good shouting abuse at people who misgender others; that is likely to end in the person being removed from the shop with more attention being brought to them and isn't constructive, nor does it build confidence in challenging people appropriately.

We need to remember that not all transgender men will choose these methods to present themselves to the world and that is absolutely fine. The main thing to remember is that these are the things that are considered safest to do if young people do wish to engage in them and that we have highlighted the issues that they may face in doing so. It does not make people any less trans or any less of a man to not do some of the things that are listed above. We need to encourage individuality, comfort, identity affirmation and exploration in order to help young transgender men develop in a safe and healthy way.

# ▌ Chapter 5 ▌

# PHYSICAL TRANSITION

Physical transition is the process by which a transgender person will seek to change their body using surgery. Some have both top surgery and lower surgery and some have only top surgery. Not every transgender person will seek surgery in order to transition; some people don't use it at all. All of these options are fine; no one is under an obligation to have surgery just because they have come out as transgender. Some individuals will need it, others will not, and that's OK. Opting for surgery is a big decision to make, so it's important that people conduct research and take their time in order to ensure that they have made the right decision for themselves.

Once a young person has made the decision to start their physical transition it is important for them to understand how to get the right support from medical professionals in order to start this process.

The main stages of transition for transgender men are:

1. appointment with GP – obtain referral to the gender identity clinic (GIC)

2. initial GIC appointment

3. three assessment appointments

4. hormone therapy

5. two assessment appointments for top surgery

6. top surgery

7. two assessment appointments for lower surgery

8. lower surgery.

## ACCESSING THE GENDER CLINICS

The first thing that a trans person needs to do is to see their GP. It's important that the patient is focused on what they want to receive out of the appointment: ultimately the referral to the GIC. The GP may ask questions generally related to why a young person feels they may be transgender. As referrals to gender services aren't something that the GP will do on a regular basis, it may be that they don't have any up-to-date information on how to make the referral or what the procedure is, so encourage a young person to take some information with them (see the Additional Information section about NHS treatment guidelines).

It may be that the GP has worked with a transgender person before and understands the process fully. However, if they don't, it's important that a young person knows their rights in relation to obtaining treatment from any NHS GP surgery and knows how to assert these in an appropriate way as some GPs have refused to treat transgender patients.

Current NHS legislation (England) dictates that young people will have patient choice as to which gender clinic they wish to be referred to. Any young person under the age of 18 will need a referral to the Tavistock and Portman Clinic. There are currently two in Great Britain based in London and Leeds. Children and young people can choose which clinic that they want to attend and have their referral sent there. Young people aged 17 can still be referred to the children's gender clinic (depending on the first appointment wait time) and then have their referral transferred to adult services from there.

According to the NHS England website, the current waiting time for the Tavistock and Portman Clinic (correct as of

March 2017) is eight months from receipt of the referral. So, children and young people will wait approximately eight months from seeing their GP to seeing a doctor at the clinic. The children's clinic is commissioned to work with young people up to their 18th birthday.

The children's gender clinics are a multi-disciplinary team that provides a holistic approach to gender dysphoria. Children and young people will receive support from a variety of professionals including clinical psychologists, counselling psychologists, systemic and family psychotherapists, child and adolescent psychotherapists, social workers, child and adolescent psychiatrists, paediatric endocrinologists and clinical nurse specialists. At this clinic, a young person will receive a diagnosis of gender dysphoria after being assessed by professionals within the team. It is important that clinical staff get this diagnosis correct and therefore treat the right issues; this is why there is a multi-disciplinary team, in order to establish whether or not there are other reasons for depression, for example. Correct diagnosis is imperative for the wellbeing of a child or young person. If they are misdiagnosed with gender dysphoria, this will cause significant issues for the young person in the long run and have an impact on overall wellbeing as a result. If a young person is in local authority care, it is important that their social worker/relevant and appropriate professional attends the appointment with them; this will help the clinical team gain an alternative perspective into the life of the young person and they may be able to provide relevant information that will help form a care plan for the young person. The initial appointment will be centred on gaining an understanding of why the young person feels they may be transgender and what the clinic can do to support them through transition. The clinic can also give advice to the parents/carers of the young person as to how they can support them if they are concerned they have gender dysphoria but are too young to voice this just yet. It may be that the child is young enough that they get upset at the thought of wearing clothes that are female clothes and they may be showing signs of distress, upset and aggression at the thought of doing so; therefore the clinic can help to provide essential advice as to what can be done to ensure that the mental health and emotional wellbeing of a child is preserved. It is important to note that, as frightening as it may be for a parent/carer of a young child who is expressing these emotions to consider a referral to a gender clinic, nothing will happen that the parent or child does not want to happen. The initial appointment will help the parent/carer gain an understanding of gender dysphoria and how they can support the child to reach their full potential and grow in an emotionally healthy way. Fear is a very real emotion, but reassure those you are working with that the appointment is a way to get advice from a trained professional who works within gender identity services and therefore could prove to be very valuable in the future.

Young people aged 18 and above will require a referral to the adult gender clinics, and the wait times from referral to seeing a doctor vary massively from clinic to clinic. The current trend is that waiting time is increasing at the gender clinics as more and more people are requesting referrals to clinics. Young people have a choice of where they wish to be referred to and can access the following clinics (see the Additional Information section for contact details and addresses):

- London and the South East

  - Tavistock and Portman Gender Identity Clinic for Adults

- The North

  - Sheffield Health and Social Care NHS Foundation Trust Gender Identity Service – Porterbrook Clinic

- – Leeds and York Partnership NHS Foundation Trust Gender Identity Service

- – Northumberland, Tyne and Wear NHS Foundation Trust Northern Region Gender Dysphoria Service – Benfield House

- The Midlands

  - – Northamptonshire Healthcare NHS Foundation Trust Gender Clinic – Danetre Hospital

  - – Nottinghamshire Healthcare NHS Foundation Trust – The Nottingham Centre for Transgender Health

- The South West

  - – Devon Partnership NHS Trust West of England Specialist Gender Identity Clinic – The Laurels.

Before a young person attends their GP to request their referral, they should have a good idea of which clinic they wish to be referred to; this will save time and help the GP to send the referral faster to the clinic of their choice.

In order for young people to make the decision as to which clinic they want to be referred to, you may want to help them consider the following:

- Which service has the lowest waiting time?

- Which service am I likely to be able to get to easily?

- Can I afford to get myself to the gender clinic every few months consistently?

It is important to remember that some young people may be eligible to claim back their travel expenses through the NHS Low Income Scheme. Generally, those who earn less than £16,000 or who are in receipt of benefits can apply to the scheme for help. This applies to parents of children who are attending the children's gender clinic also.

Having this information may give a young person the opportunity to be referred to the gender clinic that has the shortest waiting time rather than the one that is closest to them. It is important to consider that travelling over long periods of time to the clinic and over the course of a few years can be tedious in itself, so the decision to be referred to a particular clinic with a lower waiting time needs to be considered carefully for this reason.

If appropriate to your service, provide a phone line for a young person to use so that they can contact each of the gender clinics to find out what the current waiting time is before they attend their first appointment with the GP. Coach them on what to say; it is often very daunting for a young person to use the phone and speak to professionals, so when they have made the decision to progress with their physical transition, it will be a time of excitement, anticipation, worry and possibly fear, but it's important that we encourage choice and encourage young people to take control over their own transition. They will need to liaise with these professionals over the course of the next few years and possibly when they are no longer accessing your service, so providing them with the confidence they need to phone clinics will help them to develop personal skills in managing their own health care in the future.

If young people are in a position whereby they or their parents/carers can afford private gender identity service clinics, then this is also an option. One of the main things to consider about accessing private gender clinics is the cost. This will need to be taken into consideration, because the cost can accumulate quite rapidly, and if a young person runs out of money part way through their transition and needs to continue transitioning, they will have to obtain a referral to an NHS gender clinic, which will be time consuming due to the volume of people already accessing the services and lack of clinics to meet the demand.

There is currently only one private gender clinic that young people aged 18+ can access privately (see the Additional Information section for contact details):

- Gender Care – London.

Young people can also consider shared care. This is the process by which a private gender clinic will share the treatment of the patient with their NHS GP, so for example once a young person receives authorisation to start hormone therapy through their private gender clinic, the GP has agreed to provide the prescription. This needs to be approved with both the private gender clinic and the GP, and it is always better to have this approval before attending the private clinic initial assessment appointment so that you can use that time to discuss shared care before proceeding.

The following is an estimate of the costs of the first referral and assessments from a private clinic. It is important to contact private clinics directly for up-to-date prices; this is a rough guide only:

- first assessment/initial consultation – £200 to £280 (may require a non-refundable deposit to be made)

- follow-up consultations – £100 to £150.

The main benefit of using a private practice to transition is that the wait times are significantly lower, resulting in young people being able to transition a lot faster.

## STRATEGIES FOR COPING WITH LONG WAIT TIMES FOR TREATMENT

The wait for NHS treatment can significantly impact on a young person's mental health and emotional wellbeing because, at the time they have decided that they wish to proceed with physical transition and have made some efforts towards social transition, they will feel ready to take the next step towards progressing with physical transition, so waiting up to two years for an initial consultation with a gender clinic can be very difficult and does take its toll, especially if they are binding on a daily basis, because this, as discussed in the social transition section, can lead to pain and discomfort regularly which would impact on anyone's mental health.

If the young person is likely to be a service user with you for the duration of the time that they are waiting for their initial consultation, it may be important to plan ahead in order to preserve and promote positive emotional and mental health. It is likely that if you already have a support plan or care plan in place then the work you do regularly will complement the work you may do in supporting a young person throughout the time they are waiting.

Many of these are strategies that you may already know and have found useful in the past:

- Focus on what interests the young person: sports, music, dance and so on. Are they willing to join a group and focus their energy on the activity? This will enable them to feel that time is moving a bit quicker and that they are closer to their appointment.

- Planning – use a journey planner by writing down the things that the young person wants to achieve in the time frame before they attend their first appointment. This could be things relating to transition such as changing their name, coming out to their family and friends, buying new clothes and so on. Plan it out and make it SMART, therefore achievable. Celebrate each milestone!

- If a young person already has some issues such as self-harm or mental health-related issues, write a support plan around this. Encourage engagement with outside agencies specifically for these needs and write a goal-oriented person-centred plan on what they want their lives to look like at the time they reach their appointment.

- Is there something a young person has always wanted to try or do or learn? This will be the perfect opportunity to do so.

- Utilise support from trans-specific support groups. By utilising a trans-specific young person's group, young people will be able to meet other transgender people who will share tips for how to maintain optimum health and how to ultimately deal with the issues that life as a trans man can bring in a safe environment.

- Crisis planning – similar to safety planning in previous chapters, young people should be aware of what services they can access outside of normal office hours if they need support. Phone numbers for services such as the Samaritans are useful. The charity Mind has just launched a national helpline number for transgender people needing support with their mental health following a successful pilot of the project. You can find information on this in the Resources section at the end of the book; it is a useful tool for young people when other professionals/people within their support network aren't available.

It's important that young people remain healthy during the waiting time until their first appointment, because when they reach their first appointment the gender clinic will ask them questions related to whether or not they are living in role and have socially transitioned and what their mental health is like. The gender identity clinic does like to see some mental health stability in order to deal with the challenges that physical transition brings. If a young person does not have stable mental health it is likely that this will hold them back in terms of whether or not they will be able to start hormone therapy. That is not to say that the gender clinic will not support a young person with their mental health issues; they will form a plan of action for them and work towards that alongside providing support, advice and guidance on time frames and what the expectation is before hormone treatment or chest surgery referrals commence. The waiting time between the GP appointment and the first gender clinic appointment is a golden opportunity for a young person to stabilise their lives if necessary, develop healthy coping strategies and be in a position whereby they will be able to cope with the demands that physical transition puts on people.

One of the best models of practice that I can recommend and that I have used with young people struggling with low-level mental health and emotional wellbeing issues is the 'Five Steps to Mental Wellbeing' model, which was developed by the Department of Health (2017).

The five steps model is designed to support young people in strengthening their mental health by using five key steps, which are as follows:

- **Connect** – engage with people around you, in your life, or make new friends (the perfect opportunity to join a trans support group).

- **Be active** – incorporate exercise into daily routine; people don't have to run for miles on end, but maybe walk to their friends' houses, to support groups, to the shops and so on. Or it could be seen as an opportunity to try a new sport!

- **Keep learning** – encourage learning at every moment of life; learn about anything and everything. It doesn't have to involve sitting in a classroom; it could be learning about themselves, nature or trans issues, or concentrating on their college/school work. It can literally be any form of learning; it doesn't have to be formal.

- **Give to others** – supporting someone else or volunteering at a local charity that young people are passionate about helps to engage them with others, increase socialisation, give purpose and so on. This would be a great opportunity for a young person to re-engage with the community. Maybe volunteering in a field that interests them could help progress with a career in the future.

- **Be mindful** – encourage reflective thinking; encourage young people to discuss the things they enjoyed the most about their day, or the things that really mattered to them. It can literally be the smallest of things, but a reminder of these and vocalising them can help to increase self-esteem and confidence. Every time the smallest positive thing is mentioned and recognised for people with mental health issues, the more progress people make in the long run. The small achievements make up the bigger picture!

I have used this model in my own practice and have seen young people's mental health improve over time. It takes perseverance but it can be incorporated and used with a variety of issues. It could be that if a young person does want to go to a trans support group, learn more about being trans and meet other trans people and learn about their own identity then you can create a support plan around trans identity using this model. It doesn't have to be based solidly on trans issues; it can be used as a general day-to-day support plan, but it is a good place to start for increasing resilience and stabilising mental health.

## THE ASSESSMENT PROCESS

Once a young person's referral to the gender clinic has been received and the clinic is in a position to offer an initial appointment, they will send out some questionnaires that need to be returned to the gender clinic prior to the appointment. This is an important part of the assessment process. It is important at this stage to note that if a young person does move address, they must update this directly with the gender clinic, and not just with their GP. Failure to do so may mean that they miss their initial appointment and they may have to wait another significantly long period before being offered a second one.

The questionnaires are designed to understand the young person and their situation as fully as possible, and some are for research purposes. It's important that each questionnaire is completed honestly, and that each form is read properly. Some parts have to be filled out, whereas others are optional. The gender clinics are not there to catch people out as per some misconceptions; they are there to support people through their transitions and to safeguard people from harm.

The questionnaires are as follows:

- experiences of transphobia

- Rosenberg Self-Esteem Scale

- Body Image Scale

- Multidimensional Scale of Perceived Social Support questionnaire

- Inventory of Interpersonal Problems – based around social experiences with other people

- Hospital Anxiety and Depression Score questionnaire

- Autism Spectrum Quotient (AQ) questionnaire

- Transgender Congruence Scale

- Gender Dissonance Severity Scale

- Self-Injury questionnaire

- Informed Consent paperwork (to use the above information as disclosed in the questionnaires).

The assessment questionnaires come with explanations as to how the information will be used and for what purposes. It is advised that a young person completes all sections prior to their initial appointment; this will encourage engagement with the gender clinic, and if they do have any questions, they can discuss them further with their clinician at the first appointment. If a young person struggles to complete the questionnaires, contact the gender clinic. They can arrange for the booklet to be more accessible or for the questionnaires to be completed verbally at the appointment.

The first appointment at a gender clinic can be a very daunting prospect; it's all very new and a young person's journey is just beginning. It is likely they will be anxious about the appointment and will have a lot of questions that they might forget when faced with a clinician. Encourage the young person to start to compile a list of questions a couple of weeks before they attend their first appointment; they can take a notebook with them so that they can make notes of the answers to their questions. This will help ease anxiety for their next appointment and enable them to understand the process of assessment both in the short and long term.

Make sure the young person knows the address and contact numbers of the gender clinic and, if possible, do a 'dummy run' of the journey to the clinic. This will also help to ease anxiety; it can be a very stressful time attending the gender clinic for the first time; knowing where they are going can help reduce levels of stress.

Clinicians will ask young people questions based loosely around their identity, their support networks, what they want to achieve from attending the gender clinic and where they see themselves in a few years' time in terms of their gender expression. They'll discuss mental health and emotional wellbeing as well as any physical health issues.

After the initial appointment, the young person is usually given an appointment to return to the clinic and is seen by a separate clinician who asks similar questions to those described above. The point of this is that the young person is assessed by two separate doctors and then their case is discussed to identify whether or not the gender clinic is the right service for them and to start developing a support and treatment plan if applicable.

Once the second appointment has been conducted and the clinicians have both agreed that a diagnosis of gender dysphoria is appropriate, the young person will be asked to come back into the clinic to see both clinicians at the same time, and are usually asked to bring someone with them such as a friend, family member or partner. It can be a professional if the young person is in local authority care. The clinicians will ask this person questions around what changes they may have noticed in terms of the patient's happiness or any issues that have come up. It's an informal process and is solely there to add an additional level of support for the young person. Information provided can help to formulate a treatment plan and establish support networks.

At the third appointment, discussions usually start around the treatment plan, as discussed in previous appointments. The young person will have a good understanding of what will happen next depending on what they hope to gain from accessing the gender clinic. It could be that a young person wants hormone therapy and top surgery, no hormone therapy and just top surgery, both top surgery and lower surgery, or hormone therapy, top surgery and lower surgery. So it's at the third appointment that, if a young person wishes to start hormone therapy, the clinicians will again discuss this with the patient, take some time out of the appointment to discuss commencement of hormones as professionals and decide whether or not the patient is in a position to start hormone therapy or if further support is deemed necessary before that decision is made. If both clinicians agree that the patient is in a position to start hormone therapy, they will come back with consent forms and go through these with the young person, thus starting the process of a prescription being sent to their GP and the commencement of hormone therapy. It may be that the clinicians feel that more support is necessary before they agree that a young person is in a position to start hormones. This may be for a variety of issues such as unstable mental health, for example. If this happens, make sure that the young person fully understands what the gender clinic expectations of them are, because this will also help you to form a support plan outside of the gender clinic in order for the young person to reach their desired outcome. If a young person isn't able to clearly give you the information that the gender clinic has advised, you can call the gender clinic with permission from the young person to gain further clarification. It's important that if you are supporting a young person through transition then you understand the expectations the gender clinic has, because this will help you to work alongside them to stabilise young people's mental health and develop a support plan that will encourage motivation and development in order to ultimately achieve their transition goals.

## HORMONE REPLACEMENT THERAPY

Many transgender men choose to engage with hormone replacement therapy in order to help them appear more masculine through the physical changes that testosterone brings.

Not all trans men wish to take hormones; it does come with risks and permanent change, so it is a decision that must be made knowing the full extent of the impact that taking hormones will have on the body. Permanent means permanent. If a young person takes testosterone for six months and then decides that it is no longer for them, the changes they have incurred as a result of testosterone within that six-month period will be permanent; stopping taking testosterone does not remove its effects.

At the third gender clinic appointment, the clinicians will go through the consent form which highlights the risks associated with taking hormone replacement therapy with the young person. They will also identify the dose of testosterone that they feel is most appropriate and discuss different methods of administration of the drug. Some methods work better than others, depending on the individual, so it's important to consider what might work best for a young person at this point based on their identified needs (see the subsection 'Administering hormone replacement therapy' in this chapter for more details).

The gender clinic will discuss with patients the important issue of whether or not they wish to have biological children. This is a big decision for a young person to make and one not to be undertaken lightly. It can be tempting to decide not to store eggs, because the wait for hormone therapy in the first place is significant and having to freeze eggs would push hormone therapy back further until that process is complete. However, workers have a responsibility to encourage young people to think about the consequences of not doing so. As a young person, thinking about having biological children can be daunting and something that they may not have ever considered, seeing it as something to decide a lot later in life. Encouraging young people to consider whether or not they would be happy not having biological children is a necessary conversation prior to attending the third appointment at the clinic. This will put them in a position whereby they have had enough time to think about the consequences of not freezing eggs, if they choose not to and therefore help them be more prepared and confident in their decision to proceed with hormone therapy. Not every young person will want to store eggs, and that is a decision they have to make on their own. Once hormone therapy starts, it can leave people infertile, so if a young person does decide in the future that they want biological children, it may not be an option for them if they haven't had their eggs frozen.

The main risks associated with taking hormone replacement therapy are:

- blood clots

- gallstones

- weight gain

- acne

- hair loss from the scalp

- sleep apnoea

- loss of fertility.

The following side effects are generally regarded as positive effects of taking testosterone:

- increased body and facial hair

- more muscle

- clitoris growth

- an end to menstruation

- increased libido

- deepening of the voice

- redistribution of body fat.

NHS England identify that there is still some uncertainty about the possible risks of long-term exposure to taking testosterone, and the risks that are currently known to clinicians are explained fully prior to signing consent forms. Although a young person can be eager to start taking cross-sex hormones, it is important that the risks and side effects are fully understood and that they have the capacity to make this decision themselves. As discussed earlier, changes are permanent, so it is not a decision to be taken lightly.

Young people can only commence hormone therapy once they are over the age of 16; this is currently the medical standard that the NHS Guidelines work to (NHS England 2016). Prior to the age of 16, if young people are attending the children's gender clinic they can be prescribed with hormone blockers. Hormone blockers, for a transgender male for example, would cease the production of oestrogen and, if taken prior to puberty, stop puberty in its tracks. Trans men will therefore not experience a typically 'female' puberty, which can reduce dysphoria and encourage positive maintenance and preservation of mental health. Often, once puberty starts for a young person, growing breasts, starting periods and so on can contribute significantly to a decline in mental health as their body is not producing results that they would expect through puberty because of their identity as a man. Hormone blockers can be very effective at giving a young person time and opportunity to think about cross-sex hormones for the future. It allows time to conduct personal research into other people's experiences of starting hormone therapy, enabling a more rounded education on the subject, so that when they reach their 16th birthday they have made a decision based on research, publications and others' experiences without experiencing the 'negative' effects of female puberty. If hormone blockers are stopped and cross-sex hormones are not taken, female puberty would still commence.

As we've discussed already, waiting times for treatment from gender clinics are increasing, and this can leave young people without access to medical transition support. As a result of that wait time, young people can become increasingly frustrated at the thought of not only having to wait for their first appointment with the clinic, but then having to complete three assessments that are usually three months apart. Even though the assessment procedure is absolutely critical to obtain a correct diagnosis of gender dysphoria, it can feel that transition is being delayed despite young people knowing in their heart of hearts who they truly are. This can lead to them searching the internet and other sources and discussing in chat rooms how they can obtain cross-sex hormones earlier. More often than not, when people start opening these discussions on a platform whereby information is so easy to gather, young people can start to learn about obtaining testosterone through the internet. This is a particularly dangerous practice.

It may seem that taking testosterone, as other cis men often do, isn't a big deal when you compare it to other illegal substances that young people have access to; however, the damage to health that this can cause is significant. Testosterone is a controlled drug, one that is therefore prescribed by doctors who understand the effects that it will have, and should only be taken after being prescribed to a patient who understands the impacts of taking it.

When young people start hormone therapy in a controlled environment (through the gender clinic) they are supervised in doing so and are asked to obtain blood tests on a regular basis in order to ensure that the drug is not damaging their body. Endocrinologists check the blood results and discuss whether or not there should be a decrease in prescription or an increase based on their findings. Testosterone can damage the liver, and so it's important that blood tests are obtained regularly and that the patient is being monitored consistently for signs of damage to their body.

Obtaining testosterone off the internet is a dangerous practice; people don't know how much to take and can end up being hospitalised if it is not taken correctly. Every transgender man is different. Every person produces a certain level of testosterone naturally regardless of their assigned sex, so it's important that levels are checked prior to administration of the drug and throughout receipt of hormone therapy. If young people obtain testosterone through the internet they will not be monitored for potential risks, and issues that may arise can cause significant damage to their bodies, in some cases requiring hospitalisation. In addition, when the gender clinic does come to conduct the blood tests required for starting hormone therapy, they will likely be able to tell whether or not a young person has taken testosterone and will not allow them to start taking hormones and will monitor them through the clinic until their levels reach a safe point for hormone treatment to start. This ultimately delays transition further.

It is vital that young people are educated about the risks of obtaining testosterone online without medical supervision and how this can delay their transition so that they can make an informed decision about their transition and how they move forward.

### Administering hormone replacement therapy

There are two main ways in which testosterone is usually administered:

1. gel

2. injection.

Each way to administer testosterone has its own benefits and drawbacks. Tablets are rarely prescribed, as testing found that tablets were least likely to stop menstruation.[1]

The clinician will likely recommend which process of administering the drugs is most appropriate for the patient

---

1    www.revelandriot.com/resources/trans-health

based on their assessment and preferences. Most patients don't see differences in side effects between using gel and injection.

Testo-gel is a one per day sachet of gel which is to be put onto the skin daily, after showering. The main drawback from using Testo-gel is that the patient cannot come into contact with another person while the gel is on their skin and before it dries. The gel can transfer very easily to others, thus affecting another person's hormone levels. As we have already learnt, it is important that patients who are taking testosterone are medically supervised because of complications that can occur; if gel transfers to other patients through touch, this can lead to medical complications for them. At regular intervals the clinic will ask for blood samples and will regularly write to the young person's GP requesting which blood tests are done. The letters are stored in a patient's medical notes and they receive a copy of the letter, so remembering what needs to be tested at which point usually isn't an issue. If a young person forgets to take their letter to the GP they'll have all the information there and will take blood accordingly and send it to the endocrinologist at the gender clinic on their behalf. Blood tests are used to determine hormone levels. Once the endocrinologist receives regular test results, they will decide whether or not to increase or decrease the dose of hormones given to the young person. The aim is to achieve the cis male range of testosterone depending on their age.

Testo-gel is a controlled substance; therefore if young people are travelling out of the country regularly or have plans for holidays, consider whether or not this is a realistic option. They will have to obtain doctors' letters and copies of their prescription in order to take their medication abroad.

Injections are one of the most common ways to administer testosterone. Young people who have skin conditions such as eczema may prefer to use this option as Testo-gel may not be appropriate and may irritate the skin.

The young person will have an initial blood test to determine their current testosterone levels in order to decide what prescription they will receive. Initially, patients are usually prescribed Sustanon at three-weekly intervals. A patient must have their blood checked regularly, and this must be done before receiving an injection at each interval. This is so clinicians can measure the peak and trough range of testosterone. Testosterone levels will drop nearer to the time of the next injection and will peak shortly after receiving another injection. Usually, if levels are too high or too low, the frequency of the injection will change rather than the dose. For example, if a young person is receiving three-weekly injections and the levels are too high, the clinic may request that they receive injections on a four-weekly basis. Equally, if levels are too low, they may request that the young person receives their injection fortnightly with regular blood tests to ensure that the levels of testosterone are within the normal male range.

Having to make appointments to see the GP every couple of weeks can be irritating and frustrating at times, especially once the novelty of receiving hormone treatment wears off. Young people can opt, with the GP/practice nurse's permission, to self-inject. This can help to reduce the frustration that attending the GP so regularly for injections can bring. The practice nurse, if in agreement, can teach a young person how to self-inject, and it's important that guidelines are followed and that a young person receives sharps disposal units. Testosterone is a controlled drug and needs to be used and administered properly in accordance with its guidelines, and paraphernalia must be disposed of correctly and safely.

Usually, if a young person is taking injections, once the levels of testosterone is within the male range and the clinicians have found the correct dose and frequency, they will provide young people with an option of taking Nebido, which is stronger but is taken more infrequently. Some men take it once every six months and have this injected by the GP nurse; others take it once every ten weeks. Generally speaking, people usually take it once every three months. Again, a young person is required to have blood tests, although these won't be as regular because the injections will be further apart. The main benefits of switching to Nebido are that young people won't have to go to the GP as often as when taking Sustanon. It's important to recognise that injections can be painful and some people have a fear of needles, so this option needs to be considered carefully before a decision is made. It is generally the most common way of taking testosterone on a long-term basis. It is not advisable to self-inject Nebido because it has to be injected over two to three minutes as the liquid is so thick, and is injected into the buttocks. Therefore it needs to be administered by a medical professional.

Before switching to Nebido, young people are usually given an appointment to see an endocrinologist to discuss its side effects and the benefits and drawbacks of taking Nebido as opposed to Sustanon. The appointment with the endocrinologist usually takes place at the gender clinic.

One of the questions that young people are asked prior to starting hormone therapy is whether or not they have a peanut allergy. This is because synthetic testosterone (Sustanon/Nebido) is made from using peanut oil, so it's crucial that young people are honest and disclose whether or not they have a peanut allergy, or this will cause major damage to their body. It will not prevent hormone therapy; alternatives will be sought for the young person.

It is important that when a young person starts hormone therapy they are organised and they know when to book appointments to see their nurse for their injections. This will depend very much on the availability of nurses, so ensure that they check with GP reception staff as to how far in advance they can book their appointments. It's important that prescriptions are dropped into the pharmacy in time for them to make an order. Generally speaking, pharmacies do not stock testosterone as they do other drugs and it therefore needs to be ordered. It can take up to one week for it to be ordered and shipped to the pharmacy. It is a good idea to enrol on a repeat prescription service, if one is available. This ensures that the pharmacy collects the prescription, orders it and that it is there in time for a young person's next appointment.

Work with a young person to find a way that will help them remember to book their appointments with the practice nurse. This may be having a paper calendar and writing down reminders for them to stick on their walls, or using their phone to set reminders or using a diary. It's important that the time frames are adhered to when taking testosterone because hormone levels will be affected if the drug is not taken according to its guidelines.

Starting hormone therapy can be a very exciting time for a young person. However, it is important to recognise that changes do take time to achieve; they will not grow a beard and have a lower voice overnight. It's important to be patient, so focusing on positive activities will help the young person to remain healthy both physically and mentally throughout this process. Young people start hormone therapy and it is usually for life (unless they find it is something that does not align with their gender identity and stop), so focusing on other parts of their lives will be crucial to maintaining positive mental health.

Hormone therapy is a difficult time as well as an exciting one. A young person may have significant mood swings and experience being more aggressive. An inability to cry can sometimes occur, as well as acne and weight gain. It's crucial to a young person's self-esteem that good skin care is encouraged and that young people find something that works for them. Everyone's skin is different, but caring for it properly is essential to ensuring that acne is reduced. Acne is often perceived to be something that happens in teenage years; therefore it can be quite difficult to deal with this when a young person reaches their 20s, for example, so a proper skin care routine is essential to promoting self-esteem. Testosterone can increase appetite, and if young people overeat as a consequence weight gain can happen quickly, so encouraging any form of exercise will be beneficial. It's important that young people are aware of this so that they can understand their bodies, that their appetites are increasing and notice if they are gaining weight. Weight gain can be a big issue for transgender men as some surgeons require young people to be within their BMI range for surgery. Therefore making a young person aware that they may gain weight because of hormone therapy is a good way to limit damage to their mental and physical health in the long run as it will become very difficult to lose weight further down the line, especially if they are told after their surgery consultation that they won't receive surgery until they have lost weight. Preparing for it is the best way of reducing harm to a young person. Encourage a healthy lifestyle, educating on what a healthy lifestyle consists of and why it is important to maintain a healthy lifestyle and weight especially throughout hormone treatment. The GP and practice nurse can support with referrals to dieticians and nutritionists if necessary. It can also be beneficial for young people to join a weight loss support group and engage with a weight loss programme that way. If a young person is receiving benefits and they are overweight, the local council may have a programme in place whereby the GP can refer them to the gym for free/reduced fee in order for them to have access to the gym to help with weight loss.

The more changes that occur from hormone therapy, the more a young person who has gender dysphoria will feel confident and experience an increase in self-esteem in general. Although it can be a difficult time, it can also be a very liberating one. Some young people enjoy documenting their transitions, and this can be a very useful tool for obtaining support from other transgender people and to look back on their transition to see how far they have come. If this is something that a young person is interested in doing, it is important to be aware that although it has its benefits it does also have its drawbacks. Young people can document their transition in private but can also document it in public; once they open up their lives to public media platforms they are also open to criticism. Many transgender men have used YouTube to document their transitions, which is useful for other young people starting theirs, but because it is a public platform, they are also open to scrutiny from the local public. It's important to recognise this and for a young person to understand that not every member of the public will be supportive of their transition. There's a possibility that their friends and family may not be supportive and they may receive abuse online, so it's a decision that must be made in the full knowledge of the benefits and consequences of doing so.

Hormone therapy can be a very liberating time for a young person. They're finally on their physical transition and starting to think about the next steps. Encourage and support as much as possible throughout this time.

# ▌ Chapter 6 ▌

# SURGERY

Young people will need to continue to attend the gender clinic, usually at three-monthly intervals, and once hormone therapy has been started and the young person feels confident in their decision to continue with it, discussions will be had around having top surgery.

## TOP SURGERY

Top surgery is the process by which a young person has a mastectomy in order to construct a chest with a more masculine appearance. There are many benefits to a transgender young person receiving this treatment; the main reason for surgery is to reduce their dysphoria.

Not every transgender person wants to undergo surgery. It is important to understand this; you don't have to have surgery to identify as transgender. As discussed in previous chapters, it is up to the young person as to what elements, if any, they wish to pursue when transitioning, and any decisions made are acceptable. The same applies when deciding whether or not to have surgery.

A young person will need to have another assessment with two clinicians in order for a referral for top surgery to be made to a surgeon of their choice. It is beneficial if a young person starts to research which surgeon they wish to be referred to prior to attending their clinic appointments, as this will help to speed up the process.

Young people can choose to either have surgery privately or to have the procedure done under the NHS. Many surgeons offer both NHS and private options, so young people can pick a surgeon they want, and if they opt to pay for the procedure and have it done privately, they can still use the surgeon they originally had chosen, if they provide that service.

It's vital that young people do some research on each of the surgeons in turn and gain access to photos of their work; this will help them to decide which surgeon they wish to have their procedure done with. Some surgeons are better than others; some waiting lists are longer than others. There are many factors that need to be considered before making a decision as to where young people want their referral sent to.

The surgeons currently performing mastectomy surgery for transgender male patients are listed in the Additional Information section.

It may be possible for young people to access photos of their work through their individual websites; however, this is usually only applicable to the surgeons offering a private service as opposed to the NHS-only surgeons.

Many people share their before and after photos to help other people make a decision on which surgeon they would like to work with. These images are shared as part of a secret Facebook group called TMSA-UK. Many transgender men use the albums in this group to compare results from a variety of different surgeons and decide whose results they like best and therefore have their referral sent there. It is a useful tool. Please see the Additional Information section for details as to how to access the group. The group is a support network for transgender men only and is a platform for discussing worries, asking questions about issues relating to transition and specifically surgery, and gaining others' first-hand experiences.

It's an excellent way for young people to obtain confidential support from people who have walked in their shoes.

There can be a significant wait time for surgery via the NHS, and as more and more people start to have surgery, private surgeons can also have significant waiting lists. It's advisable to contact each surgeon to ask what the waiting time is; this will help young people make their decision on who to be referred to.

Transition can be incredibly frustrating, so when the time comes that a young person is looking at top surgery, it can be tempting for them to make a decision based purely on waiting times. Also, because of the pressure and pain of binding on a daily basis and the difficulties in general that transition brings, it's easy to forget about the long-term consequences of surgery when deciding who to be referred to. A young person needs to be aware that some surgeons are better than others, some surgeons have more consistent results than others and some surgeons have better results in terms of minimal scarring than others. The young person must be able to deal with the fact that their scars will look a certain way or their results may not be the best results if they base their decision solely on the wait time. Surgery is permanent; it is something that has to be lived with for the rest of the person's life, so it's important that the right choice is made.

There are four key appointments that young people will attend when they have started their journey to physical transition and are starting to engage with medical professionals for the purposes of obtaining surgery. These are the consultation, pre-operative appointment, surgery and the post-operative appointment.

## Initial consultation

Young people will be invited to attend a consultation with the surgeon at a mutually convenient time. It is at this appointment that the surgeon will be able to answer any questions the young person may have about their procedure. The surgeon will examine the young person's chest so that they can determine what type of procedure the young person is most likely to need and they will discuss the procedure and the technique with them. It is likely that if the young person has conducted some research prior to attending their appointment, they will have a strong understanding of what procedure they are most likely to have and what it involves. It is advisable that they write down questions they would like to ask the surgeon with regards to the procedure itself, healing times, what activities they can do within certain time frames and so on. Surgeons are used to people bringing lists of questions, so encourage this. Note taking while in a consultation is also common practice. Make some time to sit with a young person prior to them attending their consultation to conduct some research with them and find out what they are most concerned about in order to formulate questions. It can be difficult for a young person to remember what to ask because it is an exciting time and nerves can be the focus of the day rather than obtaining the necessary information from the surgeon. This is the best way to promote preparation for surgery because the young person will have time to use this information to prepare themselves for surgery as well as they possibly can.

The surgeon may ask to take photographs of the young person's chest with their consent; this is usually for their portfolio, for instance on their website. The surgeon takes a photograph before and after for comparison, and it is important a young person understands they do not have to have these photographs taken if they do not want to. It is not a requirement for surgery. The surgeon will go through the potential risks of the procedure and will ask questions relating to whether or not the young person smokes, their weight, their lifestyle and so on. It is advisable that a young person quits smoking in the months leading up to surgery. Some surgeons insist that a young person has to be a non-smoker for the procedure; smoking is one of the main causes of infections and can affect the aesthetics of the procedure. Some surgeons will insist on conducting a smoking test prior to surgery, and if the young person is found to be a smoker based on the results of the test, the surgeon will insist that they quit smoking before they come back for the procedure. This can push back physical transition by a significant time frame. Some surgeons also insist that young people cannot use e-cigarettes; however, others don't. It is important to carry out research on surgeons, smoking, weight and eligibility for surgery as soon as possible, because if there are things that young people do need to change about their lifestyle, starting early will promote a smoother transition process and young people are less likely to be told that they cannot have surgery due to lifestyle choices.

### Pre-operative appointment

The next stage of a young person's surgical journey is the pre-operative appointment. Depending on the surgeon a young person is using, they may request to see them at the pre-operative appointment as well as the pre-operative nurse. This is an opportunity for a young person to go through the procedure again and ask any questions that they may not have asked in the consultation.

Young people will need to complete a questionnaire while they wait for the pre-operative nurse. It's important to recognise that if a young person needs support with reading or writing someone should be with them to support them with this. If a young person has to attend the appointment on their own, it can be useful for them or a support worker to contact the hospital prior to attending to inform the nurse that they struggle to fill out paperwork. The nurse will compensate for this and go through the forms verbally with them. The questionnaire asks questions with regards to general health, any surgical procedures a young person may have had in the past, medical health, any medications a young person is taking, any allergies and whether or not they have any metal in their bodies, including piercings.

The pre-operative nurse will request that blood is taken at this appointment, as well as carrying out a urine test. An MRSA test is usually done too. The nurse will swab the inside of the patient's nose and will request that they swab the inside of their groin. The nurse will provide appropriate guidance as to how to do this and will inform the patient of anything they need to avoid or do prior to admission to hospital.

It is at the pre-operative appointment that a young person will need to purchase their post-operative binders. Depending on the surgeon that a young person uses, some may charge, others may not; also some may dictate that a young person uses post-operative binders, and others may not. It is important to be aware of this because it is advisable to take cash along in order to be able to purchase these. A phone call to ascertain whether or not they need to be purchased is advisable. Usually two binders are required at a cost of approximately £15. The nurse tends to advise that two are needed so that a young person can wear one and wash one within a 24-hour period. Again, all surgeons are different; it's important to take the medical professionals' advice.

## Top surgery procedures

There are three main top surgery procedures (Yelland 2017): key hole procedure, peri-areolar procedure and double incision procedure. The surgeon will advise a patient on the risks associated with each surgery and will give advice with regards to what type of surgery is most appropriate for the young person based on their body shape and chest size.

1. Key hole procedure: In order to have this procedure, most surgeons will dictate that breast size must be less than a B cup. It is conducted by making a small incision at the base of the areola and removing breast tissue using liposuction. Because the incision is made at the base of the areola, scarring is very well hidden and is much less aggressive. The nipple does not require a graft and therefore sensation is retained, which is better for the patient.

2. Peri-areolar procedure: The peri-areolar procedure consists of two small incisions made around the areola and for breast tissue to then be removed using a mixture of liposuction and scalpel techniques. Nipples are not grafted and do not need reconstructing, scarring is minimal and sensation is mostly retained, more so than the double incision procedure. Generally speaking, this is one of the most desirable procedures because of the scarring being less aggressive.

3. Double incision procedure: This is usually recommended to trans men who have a breast size of C cup or above. The procedure consists of two horizontal incisions made along the line of the pectoral muscle. The areolar and nipple are removed, reduced, reconstructed and repositioned in order to create a more masculine-appearing chest. This procedure leaves significant scarring and, because the nipple has to be removed and grafted on, can result in loss of sensation to the nipple.

Surgeons use these general procedures but will have their own way of promoting healing. For example, some surgeons use surgical drains designed to drain the fluid build-up from the chest that the patient will have to wear for a period of time after surgery. Other surgeons use compression binders to reduce and break down the fluid. It is imperative that young people understand the procedure they are going to have and have researched their surgeons and made a decision as to who they think will be able to provide them with the best results. Young people can opt to have their procedure privately; this will reduce the waiting time for surgery. However, they will still need to have a referral from the gender clinic in order to obtain surgery. Young people cannot just approach a surgeon, obtain a quote and have the procedure; they must be assessed as part of the gender clinic's assessment procedure prior to being eligible for surgery.

Surgery prices can vary from surgeon to surgeon, and it is advisable to contact the surgeon's office in order to obtain a quote as prices can also change year to year. A rough estimate for a private procedure is anywhere between £5000 and £8000.

## Preparing for surgery

The weeks running up to surgery can be an emotional rollercoaster full of excitement, stress and nerves. It's important to be as prepared as possible for surgery. Most surgeons will give young people a list of things that they need to avoid; the list usually consists of blood thinning medications and herbal medications. They will also give advice as to what to expect on the day, where to be and at what time, and details of their post-op appointment.

It is important to make sure that young people don't leave everything until the last minute. Surgery is psychologically and emotionally challenging, so adding in a day's worth of shopping the day before surgery will make a young person more stressed. They need to be emotionally ready and relaxed for surgery, as this will promote healing. The health of a young person both physically and emotionally will potentially determine how well healing is achieved, and as this surgery is something that a young person will need to live with for the rest of their lives, we need to promote the best possible results through self-care.

Every surgeon will have a different list of requirements. It is advisable to follow these requirements. It's useful for a young person to take someone with them to their pre-operative appointments and to have someone who will care for them while they are at hospital, at their post-operative appointment and at home. It can be difficult to remember information given verbally at these appointments because of the highly emotive experience they will be going through at the time, so having someone there to help remember advice is useful. It can also be useful for a young person to use their phone to record conversations or write down key pieces of information at these appointments so that when they go back home after surgery they can review the information given to them about their healing process and follow the medical professional's advice.

From my personal experience, I would advise that a young person who is working, or in education or training, asks for annual leave for the week prior to surgery. This is because young people can find it difficult to concentrate at work or school in the run up to surgery because there is only a week left to one of the most life-changing experiences they are likely to have. Productivity may drop and stress levels will be high. As I mentioned earlier, it is important that a young person is emotionally healthy prior to their procedure.

It is advisable to use relaxation and meditation techniques prior to surgery. These can be introduced at any point leading up to surgery; however, the sooner the better, in order to establish a routine and ensure that stress levels remain low. Breathing exercises and activities such as yoga will help a young person to relax in the weeks leading to surgery.

There is a list available from the TMSA-UK Facebook group of things for young people to take to hospital. A lot of information from this list has come from people who have had chest surgery before. The list has been added to and changed over time to give others the most up-to-date and practical advice and techniques that others have used to make things easier for them when they get to hospital and to make things easier when young people are at home after surgery.

It is a lengthy list, so it is important that young people start to buy these items early in the weeks running up to surgery. It may be that a young person is on a very low income, so planning what they will buy and when and creating a timeline to do this may be useful. Some charities may offer free items such as post-operative binders or financial support to buy items like this. TMSA have their own buy and sell group where people do give away items for free, so it's worth looking there to save some money if young people are financially disadvantaged.

It's advisable to obtain the following items:

- Button-down shirts – t-shirts are difficult to get on post-surgery and young people will need clothes to travel home in.

- Baby wipes – patients are not allowed to soak in a bath or have a shower for one week post-surgery.

- Pyjamas and slippers for the hospital – it might be cold at night; a button-down shirt is advisable to sleep in, and slippers that have a rubber sole are best to avoid slipping.

- Underwear/wash bag/toiletries.

- Pillow – if a young person is going home by car a pillow is useful to put between them and the seatbelt; seatbelts are uncomfortable without a pillow between them.

- Light cotton t-shirt – this can be worn under the post-operative binder to help to lessen irritation that can be caused by the material and to make it more comfortable to wear the binder. It may be that a young person won't be able to wear a t-shirt until two weeks after surgery due to the restricted movement in the arms, but if they can get a t-shirt on and off with help it is advisable to wear one.

- Any necessary medications and any tablets that the surgeon has recommended to take.

- Entertainment – usually the hospital has a television and wifi access and admission is usually only for one night. Patients are likely to be very tired after surgery so may not use anything such as laptops or books to read, but it's worth taking them rather than sitting there bored.

## Post-operative care

Once a young person has had their surgery, they will be advised on what to do next. Every surgeon has their own post-operative care procedures. Some will advise what to do with the drains (if used). Others will request that the young person wears a post-operative binder for six weeks after the surgery; others may advise that a young person only wears it for one week. Each surgeon is different based on their experiences, of performing the surgery over time. They will modify their post-operative care procedures based on people's experiences, so it's important that the young person takes the advice of their surgeon. Most patients are not allowed to soak in a bath, or have a shower for one week after surgery because the dressings would come off through the steam from the water in a bath, and if showering, the power of the shower may affect the incision and/or nipple graft.

Usually a surgeon will request the post-operative appointment between seven and ten days after surgery. This is when the dressings will be taken off, staples will be removed if used and the surgeon can check the incisions and grafts for infection and healing. This is the first time a young person will see their new chest.

It can be a very emotional time for people, seeing their new chest in the mirror after going through so much already. It's a time for celebration. It's worth someone else being with the young person when this happens so that they can share this with them and take some photographs! It's a time where people feel liberated. However, it's an appointment that goes very quickly because of the intensity of emotion; it can feel like it was only a few minutes long!

The surgeon will advise on what the young person can do next in terms of when they can have a shower/bath, when they can go swimming and what to look out for in terms of infection and how to obtain help and support for that if needed. Having someone with the young person at this appointment is important because of all the advice and information the surgeon will give the young person about after care. It's not very easy to take in the surgeon's advice because of the high intensity of the young person's experience of seeing their new chest for the first time.

Once the post-operative appointment is over and the young person goes home to recover, it can be a very stressful time, with the person focused a lot on the healing of their chest and worry that their nipple grafts may not have taken, that there might be an infection or that they may stretch too much and cause keloid scarring. It's quite an intense and stressful few weeks. It's really important that young people develop a routine, especially if they are off work or school during this time, because they would usually be quite active during the day. It can be boring recovering from surgery!

In the weeks after surgery, people have a range of experiences. It can be a very emotional time while young people get used to their new chests, experiencing new things like wearing a t-shirt without a binder underneath, for example. There are lots of things young people will be looking forward to and coming to terms with. For some, emotions can come in waves of relief, excitement and sheer joy at their new chests; others feel that it's completely normal to have a newly reconstructed chest, which can lead to some young people experiencing depression. When young people have a chest reconstruction, it can reinforce their identity and make them feel powerful, but if there is little emotion around their new chest because they feel completely normal (reducing dysphoria), it can be unexpected, which can lead to young people feeling low.

The stress of not doing anything around the house or not being engaged in something positive can take its toll on young people, especially if they haven't had feelings of complete euphoria at their new chest. It can be a frustrating time. In the run up to surgery, often people will think about all the possibilities that they will open up for themselves by having surgery, such as swimming, only having to wear one layer of clothing, taking their tops off on holiday and so on. Swimming is a big deal when trans people are pre-op; it can be something that a lot of people enjoy, but for transgender people, swimming in binders and worrying about tight-fitting clothing in the pool and changing rooms can be too stressful and they refrain from doing it. When a young person has had surgery and then they can't do much because they are still healing and can't do the things they were looking forward to, it can lead to bouts of depression. People expect to be able to do all the things they once couldn't but can forget that they need to heal first!

Here are some top tips for staying healthy to pass onto the young person who is recovering:

- Do something that makes you happy every day – literally anything: playing games, seeing a friend, anything that makes you happy that's reasonable to do while still recovering – don't start lifting weights one week post-surgery!

- Read a book.

- Watch a box set or film or play on a console.

- Try to go for a walk. In the first few days after surgery this may be difficult, but even walking to the end of the street can help relieve stress and encourage circulation, which is good for healing. Having someone to go for a walk with, even if it is just round the block, can help a young person to feel safe. Choose the right time of the day to go out; rush hour, for example, will just be stressful and therefore counterproductive.

- Plan your next holiday, day out or weekend away.

- Eat at least three healthy meals a day.

- Get up early and go to bed at a reasonable time – it's very easy to start staying up later and later while recovering because of the lack of routine. Maintaining a good balance of getting up and going to bed will help when a young person does go back to work or school.

- Watch YouTube videos – plenty of transgender men have documented their transitions through using video blogs. It can be useful to see how other people are healing at different stages and can give some useful tips for healing.

- Make time to do physiotherapy exercises as per the surgeon or physiotherapist's recommendation. Build the exercises into a daily routine to optimise movement and healing. If exercises are not done regularly, serious complications can occur. Take the advice of the surgeon and make sure that physiotherapy exercises are a serious focus of recovery.

- Sleep – if you need to sleep during the day, this is advisable. You are recovering from a major surgical operation and sleep promotes healing.

- Remember – your chest reconstruction is something that you will live with for the rest of your life, so encourage healthy healing and not over-doing things. If you start to lift things and go shopping in the first two weeks after surgery, for example, you can cause keloid scarring. Arranging for food to be delivered will be useful if you have no one to care for you.

Preparing for the post-operative stages is just as important as preparing for surgery in the first place. Establishing a routine, including the physio exercises and things that make them happy, and eating healthy meals and drinking plenty of water, are all important. If a young person is alone and looking after themselves after surgery, before they come home it is useful to arrange things at arm's reach to avoid, for example, reaching up high to take plates out of cupboards, which will put great strain on the incisions. If you can arrange for someone to go to their house to do a home visit or enlist the help of one of their friends, this will encourage positive mental health as they will have someone to talk to and share things with, as well as someone to make them a cup of tea. In ideal circumstances, a young person should be cared for after surgery and someone should be there overnight if possible. A lot of things will be difficult after surgery, especially showering and even lifting the kettle to make a hot drink. Wherever possible, ensure a young person has someone to stay with them for at least two weeks after surgery.

It's important to remember that if a young person is taking testosterone and needs to have their injection done within the time that they are recovering from surgery then this will have to be arranged. Also, if a young person requires transport to their appointment, wherever possible this needs to be arranged by the people around them or by contacting the GP surgery as they may have a volunteer driver's scheme that a young person can use to get to their appointment.

Once a young person has reached their six-week recovery period, they should be able to start getting back to a normal routine, and will be able to go back to work or school, attend groups or activities and generally get back to living their lives.

It is advisable that, wherever possible, young people return to work or school on a phased return. This will help them to ensure that they are not too stressed going back and that they are gently settled back into their day-to-day lives. The chest reconstruction will continue to heal for up to two years, and as this is something that a young person lives with for the rest of their lives, it's important that they obtain the best results possible for the future. A phased return will help to ensure that a young person is not overwhelmed by going back to work or school and this will encourage higher levels of attendance in the long run. If a young person is pushed to get back full time, they may find it too stressful after having such a long period of time away from that environment.

## LOWER SURGERY

Once a young person has had their chest reconstruction, they may start to consider lower surgery. Not all transgender men will have lower surgery, and this can be for a variety of reasons. Some transgender men are not happy with the current procedures that are available and wish to wait a few years to see if medical science advances to give better surgical results for transgender men. Some men don't want lower surgery at all and had only planned to have chest surgery, and some can't wait to have lower surgery. Every person has a choice about whether or not to undergo any surgical procedures, and not everyone will choose to have surgery. However, some transgender people also feel that they have no choice but to have surgery. No one particularly wants to put their body at significant risk by opting to have surgery, but more often than not that choice is taken away from them because of the dysphoria they feel. People feel dysphoria at different levels, hence why some transgender people opt not to have surgery and others opt to have both chest and lower surgical procedures.

Currently there is only one team that provides lower surgery on the NHS and privately. The team is located at St Peter's Andrology Centre, London.

If a young person decides to have lower surgery, it is important that they conduct research into what procedure they want because the two types available are very different and each has its advantages and disadvantages. What type of surgical procedure they have will depend on what a young person wants to do in terms of being able to stand up to urinate or have penetrative sex. It is entirely up to a young person as to what procedure they want. The main criterion for having lower surgery is weight; a young person must be within their BMI range in order to qualify for the surgery. Lower surgery has a higher risk of complications as opposed to chest surgery, and so the department is very strict on young people being of a healthy weight for the procedure. The recommendations from St Peter's Andrology Centre's recommendations for weight are displayed in Table 6.1. They will not consider someone for the procedure if their BMI is over 30 or if it is under 18.

Table 6.1 St Peter's Andrology Centre's recommendations for weight

| Height | Weight (kg) | |
| --- | --- | --- |
| | BMI = 18 | BMI = 30 |
| 4'10" | 40 | 66 |
| 5' | 42 | 70 |
| 5'2" | 45 | 75 |
| 5'4" | 48 | 80 |
| 5'6" | 51 | 85 |
| 5'8" | 54 | 90 |
| 5'10" | 57 | 95 |
| 6' | 61 | 100 |

## Lower surgery procedures

The two procedures that young people can opt for are phalloplasty or metoidioplasty.

Young people will have a choice as to whether or not they wish to have a hysterectomy (removal of the womb) and ovariectomy (removal of the ovaries). Young people don't have to have these procedures, but they can often be performed within the first stage of their lower surgery.

### PHALLOPLASTY

The phalloplasty procedure consists of constructing a penis using a skin graft from either the arm or thigh. Surgeons then take another graft from the buttocks to cover the donation site. The new penis is then attached to the genital area along with the construction of the neo-urethra (the start of connecting the phallus to the bladder). This is the first procedure. The second stage of the procedure is to sculpt the testicles and connect the bladder to the phallus (in order to stand to urinate), and the third stage is erectile and testicular prosthesis. This is the procedure where a rod and implants are put into the phallus in order for the patient to be able to get an erection. The testicles form part of the pump, which is used to elevate the rod in the phallus, therefore giving the patient an erection. The testicles are also therefore used to let the air back out of the pump, returning the penis to a flaccid state (see St Peter's Andrology Centre 2017).

The main advantages of this procedure are as follows:

- standing to urinate

- locker room appearance

- ability to have penetrative sex.

The main disadvantages of the procedure are:

- limited sexual function

- number of operations required

- potential complications – the phallus dying, skin grafts dying

- scarring – particularly on the arms/thighs.

Phalloplasty is a complicated procedure; the young person needs to understand the risks associated with a procedure such as this and whether or not the sacrifice is worth the outcome. As with all surgical procedures, things can go wrong and complications can arise, and this has to be considered when making a life-changing decision such as this (Pryor and Christopher 2016).

METOIDIOPLASTY

Metoidioplasty is the alternative to phalloplasty. Metoidioplasty consists of surgeons using growth (gained from taking testosterone) to create a micro penis, lengthening the urethra so that patients can stand to urinate. The second procedure for this surgery involves inserting testicular implants, thereby creating male-appearing genitalia (see FTM Surgery Network 2017).

The main advantages of this procedure are:

- ability to urinate standing up

- maintaining full sexual sensation – some men are able to have penetrative sex

- locker room appearance

- less invasive scarring when compared to phalloplasty.

The main disadvantages of the procedure are:

- possibility of not having penetrative sex

- length of penis is usually around 4½ centimetres

- urethral complications

- loss of sensation

- inability to stand to urinate

- dissatisfaction with size or shape of penis.

### DECIDING WHICH PROCEDURE TO UNDERTAKE

Although the metoidioplasty procedure is still as complicated as the phalloplasty procedure and still has its own risks associated with it, young people need to ask themselves some important questions when deciding whether or not to have surgery and which procedure they want. It's important to consider the following:

- Do they want a penis that falls within the size of an adult male or are they happy to consider a micro penis (less than 4½ centimetres)?

- Do they want to be able to stand to urinate?

- Do they want to have penetrative sex?

- How do they feel about the scarring that occurs with the procedures?

- Can they cope with multiple surgical procedures?

- Are they willing to accept the risks?

- Are there any health-related problems that may stop the young person from having a particular procedure?

Make a list of these questions to go through with the young people you support. Discuss each of the options at length. A common tool to use when making this decision is to make a visual example, writing a list of the pros and cons of each procedure and discussing them as you go along. One man's pro is another man's con, so it's important to have discussions around each of the benefits and drawbacks of the procedure in order to ensure that young people think about each individual part of the procedure and understand well enough to make an informed decision.

## Preparing for surgery
Hospital stays for both procedures will vary; it's imperative that young people take the advice of the surgical team with regards to how long they will stay in hospital for.

As there is currently only one surgical team providing lower surgery, if young people are travelling long distances to get to London they will need someone with them. Their movement and ability to look after themselves will be limited, especially with the phalloplasty procedure, as they have to have their donor arm bandaged and elevated for a few weeks after surgery.

Arrange for someone to go to hospital with the young person, and ensure that they have travel arrangements for coming home. It is better to travel by car after the surgery, as getting on public transport will be a stressful experience and one that may leave them feeling very vulnerable around other people who may knock into them, especially if it is busy. Transport costs can be reimbursed if a young person is on a lower income. Once the young person returns home they may be visited by the district nurses so that they can check the dressings and phallus for any abnormalities. This is routine and helps to reassure young people that everything is OK, as well as identifying issues and providing support as soon as possible so that they don't get worse.

Patients must be over the age of 18 for both these procedures. Metoidioplasty also requires that the patient has been taking testosterone for two years prior to having the procedure (because the growth from the clitoris after taking testosterone provides the foundation of the phallus for surgery). The London-based team is strict on weight; the patient must be of a healthy weight for their height and within their BMI range. This is because both surgeries are complicated and come with their own risks; the healthier a young person is, the better the outcome of the surgery. Unlike chest surgery where some surgeons will operate regardless of weight, lower surgery is much more complicated and the strain on the vital organs from obesity is significant. Therefore if young people are overweight, it is advisable that they are aware of this information prior to having their psychological assessments for lower surgery at the gender clinic. That way they can start to exercise and make healthier life choices in order to reduce their weight prior to surgery. It will be disheartening for a young person who has their psychological assessments and then meets the surgical team to then be told that they cannot be added to the waiting list for surgery until they are of a healthy weight. This can affect people's mental health significantly, especially as weight loss is a lengthy process in itself requiring motivation and discipline and can be a stressful time. So to be told that you cannot have surgery until you've lost weight can be demotivating, especially if the young person is already struggling to lose weight.

Preparing for lower surgery can be a stressful time, trying to get organised and remembering to take everything you need for surgery to the hospital to make the stay a bit easier. As with top surgery, it's advisable that a young person takes some time off work or school prior to the surgery so that they can organise themselves, come to terms with what is going to happen and prepare themselves psychologically and emotionally. This will aid healing.

Some of the items that trans men have found useful to take to hospital are:

- map of the local area and city

- Oyster card (if travelling by public transport within the city)

- night clothes and day clothes (remember to consider that the phallus may bleed, so extra clothing is useful)

- underwear, socks, toiletries, slippers, hand towel, sanitary towels (this helps support the phallus on the way home and will absorb any bleeding on the journey) and baby wipes

- supportive underwear (to support the phallus, particularly if a young person is having phalloplasty surgery – this is essential for the journey home)

- entertainment while in the hospital – books, magazines, music, laptop and so on

- notebook and pen to note down any questions the young person may think of

- snacks and cordial

- chargers for electronic devices
- GP, district nurse and hospital contact details
- cushion or rubber ring for travelling back home.

It's important to remember to bring essential items to the hospital but not to overpack, as the young person will have to take their belongings home with them after the procedure, which will be difficult if they take too much with them in the first place. It is better if they are accompanied and travelling by car; however, that may not be possible, and packing light will be really important.

## Post-operative care

When patients leave the hospital and are home, they have shared that it can be difficult to do normal things such as getting out of bed because the hospital beds move up and down and can lift you so that it's easier to stand up. Encourage a young person to prepare their bed with plenty of pillows and a V pillow where possible so that they can get in and out of bed much more easily. Other trans men discuss that it can be difficult to go to the toilet because generally toilets in private dwellings are much lower than those at the hospital because the bathrooms there tend to be accessible. This is important to remember as it can be difficult standing up off the toilet. It may be advisable, where possible, to have a temporary handle installed near the toilet so that young people are able to stand more easily. Speak to the local adult social care department; they may be able to offer this service if young people meet the criteria.

Remember to advise a young person to prepare in advance for coming home as well as for the actual surgery. Put things within arm's reach, take things out of cupboards and leave them on the side, and so on.

Following successful lower surgery, young people are likely to have a further appointment with the gender clinic to ensure that they are happy with the results from their lower surgery and their transition in general. For future care, it may be that the gender clinic discharges patients from their care and they have their bloods and testosterone monitored by their local endocrinologists, or it may be that they are asked to come back to the gender clinic at longer intervals, such as in one year's time, for example. This is very much dependent on the needs of the patient, so it's important that if after lower surgery the young person has finished their physical transition and does not require any further surgical procedures, they ask at their appointment how their future care will be managed.

# Chapter 7

# STRATEGIES TO OVERCOME BARRIERS TO HEALTH CARE

When it comes to general physical health for transgender men, there can be a variety of barriers to accessing services that will increase stress and emotional distress when doing so. It's important that, as workers, we support young people as much as we can to reduce the stress and the impact that this will have on their mental health. There are many strategies that can be used to support young people accessing health care. It's important that young people stay as healthy as possible both physically and mentally when they are transitioning as it is a stressful and life-changing thing to do.

Health care can become complex when young people access gender-specific health care services such as gynaecology units, breast care units and sexual health services.

Many of these services are delivered from 'women's hospitals'. This can be a difficult barrier to overcome. It can be a stressful time for a young person having to attend a women's only hospital, for example, as young people will feel that they are women's services but they identify as male, so can cause some internal conflicts and emotional distress. It is a societal issue, and one that hasn't quite caught up yet with the rest of the world. Trans men access these services too and they should be inclusive. Unfortunately, until that happens, young people will have to use the services available to them for things like gynaecology and so on.

## GYNAECOLOGICAL HEALTH CARE

For a young person, accessing a regular smear test can be an incredibly stressful and anxiety-inducing time, not just because the procedure is very invasive, but because they will also have to sit in the waiting room with other patients, and having their male name called out in that environment can be stressful and embarrassing. Receptionists are not always trained to deal with transgender men and so can often put people on the spot and inform them they are not in the right department, which would lead the young person to have to explain their gender identity. Receptionists are usually located in waiting rooms, so other patients may overhear, and this can be the start of a stressful experience and one that puts a young person off accessing services in the first place or in the future.

Prior to appointments at services such as this, there are a few things that workers can do to help support a young person through the process. Initially, it's important to establish specifically what the young person is nervous or anxious about, so that you can discuss what strategy would support them best. It may be beneficial to call the department ahead of time and to explain that the young person attending the clinic is transgender. Ask the young person if they would prefer a different name to be called in the waiting room, or if their worker is female, there may be a possibility that they can call the worker's name and the worker can take the young person to the doctor. It is advisable that the worker leaves during the procedure to ensure that professional boundaries are adhered to; however, it may take the pressure off the young person if they don't want to use their birth name (sometimes referred to as their 'dead name', which many prefer not to use), and less attention will be drawn to them in the waiting areas.

It can also be useful for the doctor who is completing the smear test to be advised that the patient is transgender and to explain what pronouns they prefer to use. This way, the doctor is prepared to perform the procedure on a transgender man and will be aware of what pronouns to use so as not to further cause psychological damage by misgendering the person. The procedure itself is invasive enough, so if workers can support young people to be comfortable from the start of the appointment and ensure that their wishes are adhered to then the process will be much easier. This will encourage a young person to stay on top of their physical health and they won't be put off attending again. Smear tests are not a pleasant experience for anyone, but can be very damaging to transgender men because of the above issues.

The healthier a young person is, the more prepared they will be to have surgery. It would be unfortunate for a young person not to have their smear tests and then get to the stage where they are ready for lower surgery and be told that something has gone wrong that needs to be dealt with before surgery. This will put back their lower surgery procedure, which again is damaging to mental health.

## SEXUAL HEALTH

Most young people will have some form of sex education, whether it's in a youth club or a school. It's important that all young people are included in this. If a young person is attending a sexual health session that is gender specific, be aware that it may not be relevant to them and all sessions need to be inclusive. It is difficult to hold a gender-specific sexual health session and be inclusive of trans men, especially if a young person isn't 'out' to others. It can cause questions to be asked of other young men about why staff are covering issues that may seem more appropriate for a female group. Trans men are just as entitled to good sexual health sessions as any other young person, so it's important to ensure that sessions are inclusive to meet those needs. Mixed gender sexual health sessions can alleviate some of the issues that could arise with single gender sessions. This will encourage young people to learn about sexual health from both perspectives, while being discreet towards transgender men, so that they can take information from the session as they need it. If you're working with a group of transgender men specifically, at the start of the session establish what language people want to use. Some people do not want to refer to body parts by their actual names; this can be distressing for trans men and a reminder that they are transgender. If the group can agree on what names they wish to use for body parts, you can use these to ensure that young people get the best outcome from the session. No worker wants young people to leave their sessions because they feel uncomfortable, and this is a great way to ensure that everyone is comfortable with the language used and understands what words describe each section of the session you're delivering. This can also help when you're working one to one with young people, because if workers understand the language that young people use to describe themselves, it can be easier to have the more difficult conversations around accessing health care or sexual health services, for example.

Choosing contraception is a conversation that needs to be had with the gender clinic. Some forms of contraception such as the pill can affect hormone levels. It is crucial that professionals at sexual health services and the gender clinic discuss this prior to giving young people contraception such as the pill if they are taking testosterone. This can be dangerous for a young person and can cause physical health problems and counteract the impact that testosterone will have on the body.

## BREAST HEALTH

All workers should be aware of how important breast health and examination is, especially for young people. It's important that young people are aware of how to check for lumps and abnormalities so that these can be checked out as early as possible, ruling out any serious issue or treating issues promptly.

Breast care is a sensitive and difficult topic to broach with transgender young people. They have varying relationships with their chests: some are traumatised by the fact that they have breasts; others tolerate having breasts, knowing that they are planning surgery; and others don't like their chests but can deal with the dysphoria associated with it. It's important to establish where the young person that you are supporting is on the spectrum. Generally, language such as 'chest' is seen as the safest option to describe breasts for transgender men; however, ask the young person what words they use to describe their chest so that you can establish a foundation for the conversation. It can be awkward for both the worker and the young person, but establishing this at the start will mean that workers will get better outcomes from the session and young people will be given information that is relevant and appropriate for them without causing undue stress and tension.

If your service doesn't provide sexual health sessions and mainly signposts to other services, workers can phone other services (with a young person's permission) and advise them that the young person is transgender and that their service needs to ensure that they provide a specific service tailored to that young person.

We all know how important caring for our bodies is; this should be encouraged just as much for transgender men as other young people. Binding is a practice that puts breast tissue at risk, and young people can develop issues from binding. It's important that they understand the process of how to examine their breasts, what to look out for and who to get help from if they find an abnormality.

## GP SERVICES

Attending the GP can be a difficult experience for young people; GPs don't tend to know everything about every patient because of their own time restraints. This can lead to some difficult conversations, for example if a young person needs a GP's help with any issue that requires them to show private areas of their body to their GP. It may be that when a young person explains what the problem is, they find it difficult to do so and they may be misgendered by the GP based solely on the fact that the GP may not be aware that they are transgender, or doesn't have time to read their notes ahead of the appointment.

If the young person feels confident enough to explain that they are trans and to explain what issues they are having, then that should be encouraged. If they need some support in accessing the GP's help, support workers can contact the medical centre they are registered to and ask the receptionist to make the GP aware that the young person is transgender and to make them aware of what issues they are having, with consent. This can make getting the right help from the GP a much easier process for a young person. If appropriate, workers can attend GP appointments with a young person and, if they consent, it may be easier for the young person to write down what the issue is so that the GP can start the conversation. If a young person is not happy with the service that they have received, they can make a formal complaint to PALS (contact details are in the Additional Information section).

Some GP practices can be reluctant to prescribe hormones and can struggle to treat transgender patients. All NHS GP services have a duty of care towards their transgender patients. They should be seeking advice and guidance from the NHS guidelines as to how to treat transgender patients and they must prescribe hormones for those who have been advised to do so by their gender clinic. Some practices are difficult to deal with, causing undue stress for a trans patient.

It is difficult enough dealing with gender clinic assessments and obtaining treatment, without having to battle with their local GP practice as to whether they can treat a transgender patient. Trans patients have as much right to access health care through their GP as anyone else. If young people are finding they are having issues with the GP – not referring to gender clinics, refusing to prescribe and so on – it is useful to lodge a complaint with PALS. Support a young person to do this in writing and, where possible, it is advisable to change GP surgery. Some young people decide not to change GP, which is of course their decision; however, they may find that they have a battle on their hands in the meantime, which could further postpone their transition. Making a complaint and having it investigated does take time. In the meantime, if another GP surgery is prepared to treat a transgender patient then strongly advise a young person to continue with the complaint but consider changing GP.

Young people can make their GP appointments a few weeks in advance if they are experiencing an issue that does not require an emergency appointment. By doing this, young people can write a private and confidential letter to the GP advising them of when their appointment is and why they are coming to see them. This can help the GP to understand the issues that the young person is facing and they can start the conversation around the issue so that the young person does not have to. Sometimes saying the first words is the hardest part, and if the GP is already aware of the issue, this can take some of the pressure off a young person.

## ACCESSING MENTAL HEALTH PROVISION

There is currently a gap in service provision for those who identify as trans to gain access to mental health services that are holistic and specifically for transgender patients that aims to address and support people through transition. The process of transition is currently mainly medical; going through transition can be emotionally exhausting and stressful, and having services that help to address depression and anxiety specifically caused by gender dysphoria are very limited, for example.

The NHS does have a counselling service; however, this tends to be a generic service and there is limited training available for counsellors working in these environments to address transgender issues. It is a very specific and specialised area of care.

The NHS counselling service is usually a 12-week service, which is inadequate when supporting transgender patients because transition is a significantly longer process and some may need support at different stages of their transition and some may need support throughout their entire transition.

The shortfall in current provision can lead to young people being left to manage without support and this is why frontline professionals have a duty and responsibility to do the best they possibly can in supporting a young person.

There is support for mental health in terms of addressing issues such as depression or suicidal ideation; however, these services only address the actual suicidal feeling rather than the issues that cause depression for transgender patients.

Provision for such services is very much sought after for transgender patients. There is a list of therapists on the Pink Therapy website that offers information with regards to which counsellor has supported transgender patients in the past and has experience of doing so (see the Additional Information section for contact details), and this can help to bridge the huge gap in service provision. Most of these services are private services and there are costs incurred with accessing such provision. If your service can commission a counsellor to work with a young person who is transitioning, it will have very positive outcomes for that young person in the long run and will help to promote positive emotional wellbeing and overall mental health. The more holistic support a young person has while they go through their journey to transition, the healthier they will become.

If provision is limited in your area, one of the best ways to support a young person's emotional health is to encourage them to attend a trans friendly support group. Some LGBT groups lean more towards supporting LGB young people and this can mean that transgender young people don't get an equal amount of support to their LGB friends. Trans-specific support groups are a fantastic way to encourage young people to meet other transgender men who have been through transition, who have advice to give in a safe environment and who can befriend and mentor young people through their transition. Mentoring by someone who understands a young person's transition and who has been through it themselves can be one of the most appropriate ways to support a young person through their transition. Having someone that a young person can confide in who has been through the embarrassing parts of transition and who isn't afraid to share their story can be one of the best ways to promote emotional health as it gives young people a sense of belonging and understanding that they may not get from generic counselling service provision or from workers in local services that they may be accessing. Professionals can be educated in the issues that affect young people and what strategies can be used to best support them; however, if people haven't been through it themselves, they won't have that deeper understanding that young people may be able to gain from others who engage with trans-specific support groups. This experience can be invaluable to young people. Some local councils and NHS services have better provision than others. Young people are more likely to find trans-specific support groups in large cities rather than rural areas. They may have to travel to attend these groups, but the experience of having that support, while there is still such a gap in provision for transgender young people, can be the difference between a young person just surviving and reaching and fulfilling their full potential.

# ▌ Chapter 8 ▌

# CONCLUSION

As described in this book, transgender men have many day-to-day battles on their hands, from social transition, to physical transition and accessing health care, and so on. It's important that we understand that every trans man will have a different experience of transition and not all young people will find things challenging. What one young person finds difficult may be different to another, and we need to recognise this so as to not make assumptions about the care and support that the young person will need from us.

Every transgender person has a different experience of transition; it is unique to each person going through the process. Not everyone will experience the things discussed in this book, so it's important that we have built a solid and trusting professional relationship with the young person so that if we're unsure about what they are struggling with specifically relating to transition then we will be able to ask them. It's OK to not have all of the answers. Transition is a practice that is still considered very new to medical professionals and society in general, so it is understandable that we don't know everything just yet. Treat young people as individuals; ask questions if you're unsure of what's going on or are unsure about what a young person's transition consists of. Ask a young person if they mind you asking questions about their transition; this should build trust, and the more trust that a worker can gain from a young person, the more likely they are able to support them and reach the best possible outcome for them. Trans men are often side-lined within local communities and even more so in LGBT communities. Society has come to accept that women can wear masculine clothes, and often transgender men get forced into this group, leading to misgendering and dangerous situations in public spaces. Within the LGBT community, it is easy for transgender men to be misgendered because there is a more widely accepted view that many people accessing those spaces are women wearing clothes that are stereotypically associated with being male. This essentially means that the spaces that are specifically for people who identify as transgender become unsafe and threatening spaces. There is still a significant amount of transphobia within the LGBT community, which is a shocking reality. Some trans people find comfort and support in spaces that are not identified as trans spaces.

Being transgender is an incredibly challenging and sometimes dangerous identity to have. Although we, as a society, have come far in changing the law and trans people have more rights, there are still those who flee the UK in fear of their lives because of transphobia.

If given equal opportunities to cisgender people, trans people can be an incredible and powerful community. The media often portrays transgender people as a drain on society, specifically a drain on the tax payer because of the services they access through the NHS. The reality is that transgender people contribute to the system just as much as other people; they have jobs in all sectors, including as professionals, and when given the opportunity to learn can achieve just as much as anybody else. Many trans people have ambition, fall in love, have families, have jobs, contribute to society, volunteer within their local communities and so on. The more we grow to accept trans people as a valued community within society, the more wider society will benefit in the long term.

# Additional Information

## NHS GUIDELINE PROCEDURES FOR GPS WHO ARE TREATING TRANSGENDER PATIENTS

https://www.england.nhs.uk/wp-content/
uploads/2013/10/int-gend-proto.pdf

## GENDER CLINIC CONTACT DETAILS

### London and the South East

Tavistock and Portman Gender Identity Clinic for Adults
179–183 Fulham Palace Road
London W6 8QZ
020 8938 7590
www.gic.nhs.uk

### The North

Sheffield Health and Social Care NHS Foundation Trust
Gender Identity Service
Porterbrook Clinic
Michael Carlisle Centre
Nether Edge Hospital
75 Osborne Road
Sheffield S11 9BF

0114 271 6671

www.shsc.nhs.uk/service/gender-identity-service

Leeds and York Partnership NHS Foundation Trust
Gender Identity Service
Management Suite
1st floor, The Newsam Centre
Seacroft Hospital
York Road
Leeds LS14 6WB
0113 855 6346
www.leedsandyorkpft.nhs.uk/our-services/gender-identity-service

Northumberland, Tyne and Wear NHS Foundation Trust
Northern Region Gender Dysphoria Service
Benfield House
Walkergate Park
Benfield Road
Newcastle NE6 4PF
0191 287 6130

## The Midlands

Northamptonshire Healthcare NHS Foundation Trust
Gender Clinic
Danetre Hospital
London Road
Daventry
Northamptonshire NN11 4DY
01327 707 200
genderclinic@nhft.nhs.uk
www.nhft.nhs.uk/gender-identity-clinic

Nottinghamshire Healthcare NHS Foundation Trust
The Nottingham Centre for Transgender Health

3 Oxford Street
Nottingham NG1 5BH
0115 876 0160
www.nottinghamshirehealthcare.nhs.uk/nottingham-centre-for-transgender-health

## The South West

Devon Partnership NHS Trust West of England Specialist Gender Identity Clinic
The Laurels
11–15 Dix's Field
Exeter EX1 1QA
01392 677 077
www.dpt.nhs.uk/our-services/gender-identity

## Private gender clinic

Gender Care – London
Box 39
101 Clapham High Street
Clapham
London SW4 7TB
enquiries@gendercare.co.uk
Telephone messages can be left on 07805 150 909.
However, the clinic requests that email is the best way to contact them.
www.gendercare.co.uk

## NHS travel costs scheme

Information on the travel costs scheme can be found at:
www.nhs.uk/NHSEngland/Healthcosts/Pages/Travelcosts.aspx
This page includes appropriate forms to make a claim and who is eligible to claim expenses back.

SURGEONS – TOP SURGERY

**Mr Andrew Yelland** (NHS and private)
Nuffield Health Brighton Hospital
Warren Road
Woodingdean
Brighton BN2 6DX
01273 621 144
info@transurgery.co.uk
www.transurgery.com

**Miss Janet Walls/Ms Grit Dabritz** (NHS only)
North Manchester General Hospital
Delaunays Road
Crumpsall
Manchester M8 5RB
Secretary: Miss Dawn Yates 0161 720 2849
Dawn.Yates@pat.nhs.uk

**Ms Catherine Milroy** (NHS only)
St George's University Hospital
Blackshaw Road
Tooting
London SW17 0QT
020 8725 1134
Secretary email: Sharon.decoteau@stgeorges.nhs.uk

**Dr Thangasamy Sankar** (NHS and private)
Nuffield Health Leicester Hospital
Scraptoft Lane
Leicester LE15 1HY
01162 769 401
www.sankar.org.uk

**Mr Peter Kneeshaw** (NHS and private)
Spire Hull and East Riding Hospital
Lowfield Road
Anlaby
East Yorkshire HU10 7AZ
01482 764 125
www.spirehealth.com

**Professor Phil Drew** (NHS only)
Duchy Hospital
Penventinnie Lane
Truro
Cornwall TR1 3UP
01872 226 100

**Mr David Oliver** (NHS only)
Exeter Medical
Admiral House
Exeter Business Park
Grenadier Road
Exeter EX1 3QF
01392 363 534
www.davidolivercosmeticsurgery.co.uk

**Mr Miles Berry** (private only)
Weymouth Street Hospital
42–46 Weymouth Street
London W1G 6NP
020 3075 2345
enquiries@weymouthhospital.com

**Mr Caddy** (NHS only)
Royal Hallamshire Hospital
Glossop Road
Sheffield
South Yorkshire S10 2JF
0114 271 4046

**Mr Dai Davies** (private only)
Cosmetic Surgery Partners
The London Welbeck Hospital
27 Welbeck Street
London W1G 8EN
020 7486 6778
Info@cosmeticsurgery-partners.co.uk
www.cosmeticsurgery-partners.co.uk

**Ms Lena Anderson** (private only)
35 Weymouth Street
London W1G 8BJ
020 7079 4242
HSCappointments@hcahealthcare.co.uk
www.theharleystreetclinic.com

**Lower Surgery Team** (NHS and private)
St Peter's Andrology Centre
Hospital of St John and St Elizabeth
60 Grove End Road
London NW8 9NH
020 7486 3840
enquiries@andrology.co.uk
www.andrology.co.uk

## TMSA JOINING DETAILS

On Facebook, search for TMSA-UK. You will then find the secret Facebook group. People who wish to be added to the group must send a friend request to 'Scott Grant', who can be found as the administrator of the group. The young person must speak to Scott in private messenger and answer a few questions relating to themselves. This is so that the group can make a decision as to whether or not the person requesting to be added is a transgender man in need of support. Without this strict process, the group cannot remain safe from people who want to enter the group and post transphobic comments or troll the group.

## MAKING A COMPLAINT TO PALS

Patients who need to make a complaint because they have not been treated appropriately at their local NHS provision can use this website to find their local PALS advocacy service and complaints procedure: www.nhs.uk/chq/pages/1084. aspx?categoryid=68

## TRANS FRIENDLY COUNSELLORS AND THERAPISTS

Young people can use this website to search for therapists who have experience in working with transgender young people and who are local to them, including the price of therapy: www.pinktherapy.com/en-gb/findatherapist.aspx

## APPLYING FOR A GENDER RECOGNITION CERTIFICATE

Use this website to download appropriate application forms and lists of evidence that young people will need to submit

to the panel for their gender recognition certificate: https://
www.gov.uk/apply-gender-recognition-certificate

## APPLYING FOR A FREE UK DEED POLL

It is advisable to use the free deed poll service before paying for
a name change. A free deed poll is just as legitimate as a paid
one: https://freedeedpoll.org.uk

## NAME CHANGE ADVICE

Use the government's website to gain advice with regards to
how to conduct a name change: www.gov.uk/change-name-
deed-poll

# Resources

**Albert Kennedy Trust** – AKT provides support for LGBT young people who need supported accommodation that is safe. It is a targeted service that provides housing support for LGBT people only: www.akt.org.uk

**Gendered Intelligence** – specialises in supporting young trans people aged 8–25, as well as delivering trans youth programmes, support for parents and carers, professional development and trans awareness training for all sectors.

200a Pentonville Road
London
N1 9JP
0207 832 5848
www.genderedintelligence.co.uk

**GIRES** – resources and e-learning for professionals who wish to improve their knowledge on transgender issues and how to support trans people: https://www.gires.org.uk

**LGBT Foundation** – offers a variety of support such as counselling, telephone support, events and workshops.

5 Richmond Street
Manchester M1 3HF
info@lgbt.foundation
0345 330 3030
http://lgbt.foundation

**Mermaids UK** – supports transgender children and their parents and will offer support to community groups and schools working with transgender children.

Suite 5
High Street House
2 the High Street
Yeadon
Leeds LS19 7PP
0344 334 0550
info@mermaidsuk.org.uk
www.mermaidsuk.org.uk

**Mind Line Trans + support phoneline** – currently open two nights a week (Monday and Friday) from 8pm until midnight: 0300 330 5468

http://bristolmind.org.uk/help-and-counselling/mindline-transplus

**MORF** – provides support to transgender men. Also has a catalogue of binders for people who are on low incomes. Young people can pick a binder from the catalogue to be sent to them free of charge if they cannot afford a proper binder. This reduces harm from binding with materials that are not advisable: https://morf.org.uk

**Press for Change** – an organisation which supports transgender people in enforcing the law in terms of their rights and supports institutions to adhere to the law in supporting trans people: www.pfc.org.uk

**Samaritans** – suicide prevention. Phone: 116 123. Email: jo@samaritans.org. Local centres can be found on their website: www.samaritans.org

**Stonewall** – Stonewall's website provides information with regards to support that can be obtained locally by them.

The website also provides information relating to rights for trans people, reporting hate crime and how to obtain support: www.stonewall.org.uk/help-advice

**True Vision** – provides a hate crime reporting service through their website if young people are not confident in phoning the police: www.report-it.org.uk/report_a_hate_crime

# References

Brill, S. and Pepper, R. (2008) *The Transgender Child.* San Francisco, CA: Cleis Press.

Criminal Justice Act (2003) Accessed on 11 November 2017 at www.legislation.gov.uk/ukpga/2003/44/contents

Department of Health (2013/14) *Interim Gender Dysphoria Protocol and Service Guidelines.* Accessed on 10 November 2017 at www.england.nhs.uk/wp-content/uploads/2013/10/int-gend-proto.pdf

Department of Health (2017) *5 Steps to Mental Wellbeing Model.* Accessed on 10 November 2017 at www.nhs.uk/Conditions/stress-anxiety-depression/Pages/improve-mental-wellbeing.aspx

Equality Act (2010) Accessed on 10 November 2017 at www.legislation.gov.uk/ukpga/2010/15/contents/enacted

FTM Surgery Network (2017) *Metoidioplasty Procedures.* Accessed on 10 November 2017 at www.metoidioplasty.net/procedures

The LGBT Bar (2017) *Gay and Trans Panic Defence.* Accessed on 10 November 2017 at http://lgbtbar.org/what-we-do/programs/gay-and-trans-panic-defense

National Centre for Lesbian Rights (2017) *#BornPerfect: The Facts about Conversion Therapy.* Accessed on 10 November 2017 at www.nclrights.org/bornperfect-the-facts-about-conversion-therapy

NHS (2017) *Gender Dysphoria.* Accessed on 10 November 2017 at www.nhs.uk/conditions/gender-dysphoria/Pages/Introduction.aspx

NHS England (2016) *Clinical Commissioning Policy: Prescribing of Cross-Sex Hormones as Part of the Gender Identity Development Service for Children and Adolescents.* Accessed on 10 November 2017 at www.england.nhs.uk/commissioning/wp-content/uploads/sites/12/2016/08/clinical-com-pol-16046p.pdf

Peitzmeier, S. (2015) *Health Impact of Chest Binding among Transgender Adults: a Community-Engaged, Cross-Sectional Study.* Accessed on 10 November 2017 at https://transfigurations.org.uk/filestore/binding-project-postprint.pdf

A J Pryor and A N Christopher (2016) *Patients' Guide to Phalloplasty.* Accessed on 10 November 2017 at www.ngicns.scot.nhs.uk/wp-content/uploads/2016/08/Patients-Guide-To-Phalloplasty.pdf

St Peter's Andrology Centre (2017) *Operative Staging of Phalloplasty.* Accessed on 10 November 2017 at www.andrology.co.uk/phalloplasty/operative-staging-of-a-phalloplasty

Strudwick, P. (2014) *Nearly Half of Young Transgender People Attempted Suicide – UK Survey.* Accessed on 10 November 2017 at www.theguardian.com/society/2014/nov/19/young-transgender-suicide-attempts-survey

Summerville, C. (2015) *Unhealthy Attitudes Report.* Accessed on 10 November 2017 at www.stonewall.org.uk/sites/default/files/unhealthy_attitudes.pdf

UK Council for Psychotherapy (2014) *Conversion Therapy: Consensus Statement.* Accessed on 10 November 2017 at www.bps.org.uk/system/files/Public%20files/conversion_therapy_final_version.pdf

Yelland, A. (2017) *Chest Reconstructive Surgery.* Accessed on 10 November 2017 at www.transurgery.co.uk

Yeung, P. (2016) *Transphobic Hate Crimes in 'Sickening' 170% Rise as Low Prosecution Rates Create 'Lack of Trust'.* Accessed on 12 December 2017 at www.independent.co.uk/news/uk/home-news/transphobic-hate-crime-statistics-violence-transgender-uk-police-a7159026.html

# Index